Whither State Welfare?

The RIPA, founded in 1922, is the leading independent British institution concerned with policy making and administration in the public sector. Its aims are to help improve the effectiveness of public administration and to increase public understanding of institutions, processes and policies in the public service. It is concerned both with the needs of public authorities and also with the needs of the public they serve.

RIPA STUDIES

1 *Major Public Corporations: A Statutory Analysis*
   David Pierson

2 *Financing Public Sector Pensions*
   Raymond Nottage

3 *Appraisal for Staff Development: A Public Sector Study*
   Ronald Wraith

4 *The Consumer Cause: A Short Account of Its Organization, Development, Power and Importance*
   Ronald Wraith

5 *Open Government: The British Interpretation*
   Ronald Wraith

6 *The Commission for Local Administration: A Preliminary Appraisal*
   Norman Lewis and Bernard Gateshill

7 *Government as Employer — Setting an Example?*
   P.B. Beaumont

OTHER RECENT RIPA PUBLICATIONS

Allies or Adversaries? Perspectives on Government and Industry in Britain
   Sir Keith Joseph, Sir Leslie Murphy, Sir William Barlow, Alan Lord, Ray O'Brien and John Smith

Facing the Energy Future: Does Britain Need New Energy Institutions?
   RIPA Conference Proceedings

Government Policy Initiatives 1979-80: Some Case Studies in Public Administration
   Edited by P. M. Jackson

Inspectorates in British Government: Law Enforcement and Standards of Efficiency (published in association with George Allen and Unwin Ltd.)
   Gerald Rhodes

Policy and Practice: The Experience of Government
   Tony Benn, Edmund Dell, Merlyn Rees, William Rodgers and Shirley Williams

Whither State Welfare?

Policy and Implementation in the Personal Social Services, 1979-80

Adrian Webb
Gerald Wistow
University of Loughborough

ROYAL INSTITUTE OF PUBLIC ADMINISTRATION

Published by the Royal Institute of Public Administration,
3 Birdcage Walk, London SW1H 9JJ.

Printed in England by Imediaprint Limited,
1/9 Memel Street, London EC1Y 0SY

ISBN 0 900628 25 1

PREFACE

Much attention is accorded to public policy-making as a process, to the content of public policies and to the operation of the machinery of government. Unfortunately, however, the tendency is to consider policy making to the exclusion of the problems posed by attempts to enact policy, and to study particular elements of the machinery of government rather than its overall use as a means of enacting policies. The gulf can be bridged semantically by asserting that policy making and implementation are the seamless cloth of governance. What this resolution fails to reveal are the problems of translating policies into social reality. Policy implementation needs to be studied in its own right precisely in order to locate it within a fuller understanding of the policy process. In pursuing this task, we may also shed light on the nature and meaning of public policy and the extent to which it is a central or peripheral influence on the machinery of government.

This study comprises two inter-related strands: a conceptual discussion of policy and policy implementation and an outline of the 'policies' towards the personal social services — new and inherited — which characterized the period of Conservative Government up to December 1980. Both these strands are intended as a base from which, subsequently, to record the problems of implementing these policies. They are offered in this form as an attempt to 'set the record straight', descriptively and conceptually, at the beginning of what the Government intended to be a period of radical change and transformations.

This monograph is one product of a continuing project, initiated by the Royal Institute of Public Administration and supported by a grant from the Leverhulme Trust, to study the implementation of a variety of policies over the life of the Conservative Government which came to office in 1979. The initiative is a collaborative one which has already resulted in a joint publication.[1] However, in preparing our own contribution for the collaborative project, we felt that a number of issues warranted closer analysis than could be achieved in a short essay. This monograph reflects the RIPA's decision to support a fuller discussion of those issues.

The first three chapters are primarily conceptual and include a particular conceptualization of the term 'policy' and a discussion of policy implementation. The detailed analysis of changes in personal social services policy contained in the fourth chapter will be of particular interest to students of these services and to students of public expenditure. The discussion includes a typology of 'cuts' and seeks to answer the question: what is a cut in public expenditure? Chapter V is devoted to one area of policy — that of expanding 'non-statutory welfare'. This phrase has come to mean the voluntary social services and the wide range of care provided by families and neighbourhoods. The assertion that an increase in 'welfare pluralism' is needed is examined in detail. This section should be of special interest to those who are active in the voluntary sector or who have followed the contemporary policy debate on this subject. The concluding chapter contains a brief synthesis of the conceptual and descripive strands of the book and poses the question: what problems of policy implementation do Government policies highlight and how have these been, or might they be, tackled?

A.L.W.
G.W.
September 1981

Contents

I The Nature of the Personal Social Services

This book examines the nature of the present Government's policy for the personal social services (PSS) and the extent to which implementation of that policy had proceeded by the end of 1980. First, however, we highlight four features of the PSS which form the context within which policy in this field is formulated and implemented.

The location and status of the PSS in central government are important since they are greatly overshadowed, certainly in budgetary terms, by the other two areas of policy for which the Secretary of State for Social Services is responsible: the National Health Service (NHS) and Social Security. While the Department's planned total budget for 1980/81 amounted to some £28,500m (out of a public expenditure total of £74,500m), the PSS share was under £1,300m. Although still comparatively small, the PSS have since 1950 experienced growth faster than that for public expenditure as a whole or for any other social service. During the 1970s, PSS expenditure grew from 11.5% to 15.9% of the total health and personal social services programme.[2] The treatment of these two services as a single programme area for public expenditure services may in itself have implications for central government's view of policy and priorities within the PSS. Finally, it should be noted that the existence of the Voluntary Services Unit (VSU) within the Home Office with responsibility for co-ordinating central government support for voluntary action (acting as the 'friend' of voluntarism in central government) brings that Department into the PSS field.

At local level, the statutory PSS are the responsibility of local authorities. This means that policies and priorities are considered locally not in relation to the NHS but (theoretically) in relation to local services which relate to central government departments other than the DHSS. It also means that the PSS cannot be discussed without reference to the general approach to local government adopted by this administration. Finally, 'successful' implementation is dependent upon the existence of congruent policy paradigms at both levels of government.

To a greater extent than any other social service, apart from housing with its large private sector, the PSS are characterized by a 'mixed economy of welfare'.[3] The vast bulk of caring in this field is provided informally by families, friends and neighbours, while the voluntary sector is a large and growing feature of total activity within it. Indeed, the

Wolfenden Committee calculated that the total number of full-time equivalents working in the voluntary and informal sectors was greater than that employed in the statutory services.[4]

The nature of the clientele served by the PSS is the fourth important contextual factor. As Pinker has observed, this is 'largely composed of the weakest bidders in the economic market':[5] the elderly, physically and mentally handicapped, mentally ill, children 'in trouble' and families under stress. This is an important factor in view of this Government's request that local authorities should protect the 'most vulnerable' from the effects of public expenditure constraint. Another feature of the clients served by the PSS is their dependence upon an interlocking range of social service provision and their vulnerability to changes in the economic environment, especially the growth of unemployment. Constraints upon the supply of any one of the PSS, housing, health and education services are reflected in increased demand pressures upon the others. Finally, on the demand side, demographic trends among the elderly, growing numbers of children in care, and of mentally handicapped children receiving local authority services, have made necessary some measure of growth in the PSS in order merely to maintain existing standards and levels of provision.

II What is 'Policy' in the Personal Social Services?

In preparing this study, we interviewed senior officials of central and local government departments, local authority associations and voluntary organizations at central and local level. Many of them questioned whether, at that stage in the Government's life (spring and autumn 1980), there was evidence of much specific policy towards the PSS. They felt that public expenditure policies had dominated this, as all other, fields of government. While there was clearly a strong desire on the part of ministers to develop non-statutory forms of care, the officials felt that it was difficult to detect anything tangible in this area other than the rhetoric of ministerial speeches. Articles in the 'professional press' similarly expressed doubts about the nature of government policy in the PSS. Such comment focused particularly on perceived inconsistencies and contradictions in the Government's stance towards, for example, expenditure policy, protection of the most vulnerable and support for voluntary action.[6] The House of Commons Social Services Committee was similarly critical.[7] Such views raise important questions both about what we mean by the term 'policy' and also about the nature of the process by which governmental initiatives are implemented and achieve substantive impacts on the ground.

The term 'policy' tends to carry far too many and diverse meanings for analytical purposes. 'Government policy' tends to be a way of referring to all the more or less purposive attempts by governments to prosecute, or exercise influence over, changes in and pertaining to the nation state. The term policy may therefore be applied to whole bundles of objectives and stances, as in 'foreign policy' or 'economic policy'. Policy in this sense may take the form of highly generalized expressions of attitude or intention, or closely integrated networks of interlocking decisions.

Policies may therefore be categorized in terms of their specificity, their autonomy or interdependence, and the extent to which they relate to a single issue or a portmanteau of inter-related problems and issues. These dimensions are obviously linked one with another and they emphasise the importance of the perceptions of policy makers. No issue or problem can be isolated entirely from the wider social, economic and political context of society; but the more inclined a policy maker is to treat it as if it were, the more likely it is that a specific, autonomous, single-issue policy will result. Policies may also take the form of an *explicit* stance or statement of intention designed to guide decisions, or they may be *implicit*

11

and revealed only in the content and style of a decision or stream of decisions.

What remains constant in the types of policy noted above is the orientation towards prosecuting or managing change. However, apart from differences in the characteristics of policies themselves, the means of influencing change may vary widely. A policy may be intended to influence the actions of individual citizens, senior policy-makers in other countries, or entire networks of interlocking organizations and institutions comprising, for example, 'the economic system'. However, one of the most typical and common assumptions is that policies are the means of exercising control over particular organizations or, viewed differently, that organizations are brought into existence to give expression to policies. This association of policy with organizations represents a second, much 'tighter' and powerfully managerialist way of viewing the term policy.

The post-war pre-occupation with 'rational' policy-making rests on the idea that organizations are or should be *goal-directed:* that they exist to enable purposive action to be taken which will have an impact on the environment in which the organization exists — to the benefit of some, in principle identifiable, group or groups. Given the commitment to the idea of organizations as goal-directed, 'policy' is central to the legitimate exercise of control in organizations. This perspective tends to emphasise a notion of policies as explicit, specific and carefully inter-related. It favours a view of policy as *process* and not merely as statements of intent or stances, the 'implementation' of which once pronounced *ex cathedra* can be taken for granted. Running organizations on the basis of policies is a continuous struggle to obtain or retain control over the implementation of policies and the redesign of policies to ensure that they remain valid and implementable guidelines for action. Policy implementation is therefore an integral part of any study of policy.

This 'managerial' view of policy has served to link the control of organizations to the more generalized and diffuse notions of governmental policy. A commitment to rational, goal-directed, managerial behaviour readily envisages a chain of policy specificity by which broad government policies are translated into increasingly explicit, specific and closely inter-related policies assigned to particular government agencies through which they are implemented. Government policy — refined into a 'hierarchy' of increasingly specific sub-policies — is therefore the *raison d'etre* of government organizations, and government organizations are a dominant vehicle and object of government policy. However exaggerated this is as a caricature, the post-war commitment to expand the role of the state and to emphasise rational processes of management has tended to bridge the gap between the different notions of policy to which we have alluded by supporting the ideal of a highly coordinated hierarchy of policies and sub-policies as the legitimate core of state action through public organizations.

The difficulties and reservations which this 'ideal' engenders are legion. We can identify a few by means of brief questions. To what extent do governments attempt to manage change in society through government agencies and through policy making and implementation, rather than by attempting to create an intellectual and moral 'climate' which influences the values, attitudes, beliefs and power relationships of the society? How far do governments identify objectives clearly and translate them into explicit policies? Insofar as policies are developed, are they welded into integrated networks of inter-related and compatible decisions, or are they characterized by considerable autonomy and mutual incompatibility? How effective is managerial control through policy: are policies the major determinant of government agencies' outputs or are such outputs the end-product of an altogether less hierarchical and less co-ordinated form of goal-directed behaviour than is implied by the managerialist perspective? How effectively can a single policy, or interlocking sets of policies, be implemented: what, in practice, are the problems of policy implementation?

We cannot begin to address ourselves to more than a few of these questions in this book. However, the advent of a new Government committed to radical social change and to the 'modelling' of societal values and attitudes, as well as shifts in policy, presents an obvious opportunity to address some of them. The presumption that such a Government would be likely to develop new policies raises the possibility of using such policies as tracers to illuminate the problems of implementation. The approach taken in this monograph is therefore to operate largely within the general framework of the 'managerialist' view of public policy. The backdrop is an 'ideal' of an integrated framework of well co-ordinated, explicit and successively more specific government policies designed to control the output of public services and to be implemented through the organizational structures and processes of these services. This 'ideal' is merely a heuristic device. It is not assumed that governments should necessarily conform with such expectations, and one of the major points of interest is precisely that before its election in 1979 the Government had clearly indicated its distaste for the statist and the centralist features of this 'ideal'. The task facing it was therefore to effect change in society and in the machinery of government simultaneously. One manifestation of this in the personal social services was the keen interest shown in non-statutory forms of social provision, a topic treated as a 'case-study' in the final section of this book.

For the moment, however, we need to return to the idea of policy as a statement of intent and to consider a dilemma which is all too easily concealed within this simple formulation. Students of social administration have usually assumed that policy 'really means' policies about what we want to achieve by way of meeting social need. Meeting social need is taken to be the broad goal of social services, and the specification of social needs is seen to provide the objectives for particular policies. Policies, therefore, are seen to revolve around:

ideas about need;

ideas about the causality underlying need; and

ideas about attempts to reduce such needs.

The assumption that this is what policy is about is so widespread that it needs to be placed within a wider context. We prefer to call this area of policy 'service policy' or, more generally, 'outputs policy'. Our assumption is that, in practice, politicians and administrators in both statutory and non-statutory services respond to a wider variety of stimuli than those provided by social need, and that 'policy' is, therefore, an altogether more complicated matter. Specifically, we identify the following:

(a) *Governance policies* — are concerned with perceptions of the proper role of the state in general and of central government in particular; the structuring of relationships between governmental and non-governmental bodies; and the organization and management of such bodies. In the first case, in particular, we would suggest that this is an area of meta-policy which has been taken for granted by governments in the post-war welfare consensus. However, the present Government has explicitly sought to bring policies of governance to the centre of its programme.

(b) *Resource policies* — are concerned with desired levels and combinations of financial, manpower and capital inputs. Although, ideally, policy may be seen as a systematic integration of what we have called service policies and resource policies, we would argue that these largely operate in considerable isolation in practice. We therefore need to identify resource policies quite specifically.

(c) *Service (or output) policies* — are concerned with meeting social needs and include the allocation of priority to particular client groups or the specification of preferred ways of responding to need (e.g., a preference for community as opposed to residential care). They are the kinds of policy currently said to be lacking.

(d) *Policies in related fields* — include a number of, for the most part, service policies which impact upon the PSS directly or indirectly.

Identifying 'policy streams' of this kind enables us to escape from the assumption that service outputs are the primary objective of government policy-making and that organizational and resource questions will be subordinated to this primary objective. We can now envisage great complexity and uncertainty of outcome even within the rational managerialist policy perspective. If such policy streams are supported by different intellectual and ideological underpinnings and are institutionalized in different organizational processes, sub-units and professional cultures, the outcome of 'policy' is uncertain unless predominance is accorded to, or secured for, one policy stream. In short, we can argue that whole streams of policy may enjoy relative autonomy of one another, giving rise to mutual incompatibilities and unexpected outcomes, until or unless a degree of co-ordination is imposed. The different priorities and ideologies of different governments may result in a shifting balance of power/predominance between these policy streams, but it has also to be assumed that predominance may be resisted by actors identified with the subordinated streams. Conflict and competition between policy streams, as well as between specific policies within each stream, rather than policy co-ordination and a tidy hierarchy of increasingly specific policies, may therefore be anticipated as a likely possibility. In such circumstances, policy implementation may be extremely difficult and uncertain.

If we relate this categorization of policy streams to the PSS, our argument is that, currently, there is no lack of policy, merely that the governance and resource — rather than service — policy issues have been accorded prominence by this Government, though this is not to say that such policies have been fully articulated or executed. The dominance of governance, and especially of resource, policies in government thinking does however raise some interesting issues. For example, at what point should one argue that a particular level of public expenditure reduction amounts to an implicit abandonment of a particular service policy? Much emphasis has been placed in recent years on the relative priority accorded to various client groups and on the development of community-based services as an alternative to institutional and health service care. At what point does a lack of funds undermine such policies? In short, one of the problems of which we must be aware is that when, in Self's terms,[8] 'market compression' becomes an over-riding policy objective, service policies may be implicit rather than explicit and earlier service policies may be abandoned implicitly. This possibility emphasises the importance of examining how politicians and administrators respond to broad statements of central policy. Another intriguing feature of the present situation, however, is that the very approach to issues of governance adopted by the present Government makes it much more difficult for them to implement some of the changes in service policy which they should like to see achieved (e.g., a shift towards greater support by local authorities of voluntary sector activity), as will be indicated later.

III Policy Implementation

In the previous section we argued that viewing policy as a means of exercising control or influence over the working of organizations highlights the importance of policy implementation as an integral component of the policy process. This orientation has been sharply reinforced in recent years by the widespread recognition of 'policy failure': the gradual opening up of a yawning chasm between the promise and the achievement of public policy.

The problems of policy implementation therefore demand attention for good academic and practical reasons; a government dedicated to radical action based on its own distinctive interpretation of the 'policy failure' of recent decades offers an opportunity for such research. However, the relationship of work on policy implementation to the broader fields of policy studies needs to be considered at the outset. An examination of problems of policy implementation can only address itself to such questions as: given explicit policies, has the quality of 'follow through' been sufficiently good to give them a chance of making a real impact; have the problems of implementation resulted in policies being dropped or substantially modified? Inadequate implementation can be eliminated as a reason for policy failure, but the theoretical, technical and political adequacy of the policies themselves cannot be evaluated. At best, the study of policy implementation would only enable one to judge the appropriateness of a policy in terms of its ease or difficulty of implementation.

In this sense, policy implementation is an area of technical rather than political study and evaluation. Nevertheless, it is an essential element in a wider and more overtly political assessment of public policy; and implementation is itself a deeply political, as well as technical, process. The implementation of policies involves the use of power, the promulgation or reinforcement of particular values and the distribution of resources. The study of policy implementation, therefore, initially involves a willingness to disregard the question, 'Is this a good or appropriate policy? in favour of the less exciting query, 'What are the problems of enacting this policy?' This managerial emphasis in policy implementation, however, should be located firmly within a more critical body of policy studies, and contribute to it.

Having begun to map the intellectual location of policy implementation as a field of study, it may reasonably be asked: how can it be differentiated from the study of public administration in general? Compared with the tradition of institutional description and analysis which dominated public administration in the post-war years, a concern with implementation is far more clearly grounded in an interest in the *products* of public institutions and not their operation *per se:* it is policy oriented. The approach which has informed public administration increasingly since the early sixties, however, is also policy oriented. The emphasis has been on the analysis of policy formation, financial decision-making and control, quality control and redress of grievance.

How, if at all, does policy implementation differ from this processual approach to public administration? The enigmatic answer is that policy implementation is both a wider and a narrower area of study. It is wider in the sense that questions about policy implementation will inevitably spill over into many disciplines (e.g., organizational sociology and social psychology) and it is narrower in the sense that the processes of public administration are only important insofar as they are pertinent to the implementation or non-implementation of explicit policies.

This difference is crucial and it highlights the first cutting edge of policy implementation as a field of study. The question has to be asked: how far are public organizations operating to implement explicit policies, and how far are their internal dynamics dominated by quite other considerations? It is all too easy to assume that public agencies exist to give expression to policies. In practice this may be the exception rather than the norm. For example, the personal social services — or the health or social security services — are quite definitely underpinned by programmes of service production, but whether these are in turn the expression of coherent and explicit policies is another matter. As in all organizations, there is a strong tendency to routinize the production of certain goods and services without questioning their continued relevance or the extent to which they contribute to the attainment of clearly articulated policies. Policy implementation, therefore, may be quite different from *programming*. Indeed, much of the debate over incremental and rational comprehensive approaches to policy formation precisely reflects this difference between developing specific policies on the one hand and maintaining large-scale programmes of service production on the other. Let us therefore seek a conceptual framework within which to discuss the implementation of specific and explicit policies while acknowledging that such policies may have only a relatively modest impact on the way in which organizitions work.

A CONCEPTUAL FRAMEWORK FOR STUDYING IMPLEMENTATION

The implementation of a policy depends upon the successful handling of four principle areas of action which we will examine in turn:

 the knowledge, or theoretical, base;

the power, or support, base;
the administrative base; and
the resource base.

The first, in our view, is most readily overlooked and therefore merits emphasis. The inadequacy of our knowledge base in the field of cost-effectiveness has recently been highlighted by the Social Services Committee which noted that 'on the basis of the research carried out so far, the Department does not appear to be able to "draw firm conclusions" about policy'.[9] But the problem is not confined to such comparatively sophisticated issues as cost-effectiveness comparisons of different service packages. However practical and straightforward a policy may be, it rests upon some form of theoretical understanding, although this may well remain implicit and be given limited attention. Consider, for example, the provision of meals on wheels to old people. Unless it is to be regarded as a purely altruistic act (in which case it still implies the hypothesis that old people will enjoy receiving meals on wheels!), a meals service rests upon assumptions about the political or welfare benefits to be derived from such meals. The political case, which can be dismissed briefly — without implying that it is unimportant — is that meals on wheels win votes or help political parties to avoid losing them. The welfare case assumes either that without such meals old people may suffer nutritionally, with implications for other forms of service, or that the regular delivery of meals provides an opportunity to monitor the wellbeing of vulnerable people and to relieve their social isolation. The social isolation proposition further entails assumptions about the consequences of social isolation and therefore the need to intervene, as well as an implicit hypothesis that regular but brief visits can be an effective form of intervention.

The theoretical base of this simple service is therefore a complex one and has in fact been given far less attention than it deserves in the development of the personal social services. The essential components are a theory of the problem — the nature, definition, extent, intensity and distribution of malnutrition and social isolation; a theory of causality — the origins and causes of malnutrition and social isolation; and a theory of intervention — the efficacy, cost and acceptability of combating malnutrition and social isolation in different ways. In the case of meals on wheels it can be seen that there are at least two major 'problems' which can be identified and ample room for imprecision or dispute over the theoretical base of the policy. East German social policy makers, for example, view the British practice of providing meals on wheels with incredulity because they see the maintenance of an old person's social identity and place in society as far more important than simply enabling old people to continue to manage in their own homes. Consequently, meals provided communally in factories and social centres are seen as a means to a wider goal and meals on wheels are viewed as a symbol of social isolation rather than a partial remedy.

19

The power or support base of a policy depends in part on its knowledge base. Politicians and professional workers at different levels of government will withhold or give support partly as a result of judgements about the way the problem has been defined and the feasibility and acceptability of the proposed form of intervention. The progression of working papers, consultation documents, white papers and bills which precede legislation are precisely a means of gaining support as well as a means of clarifying the theoretical base of policy or, indeed, of muddying the waters of theoretical debate in the interests of gaining support. But support has also to be gained from other actors who are crucial to implementation but whose interest in the policy is largely instrumental: people who see it as a source of work to be done without identifying with its objectives. For this reason, we will emphasise below the importance of gaining compliance.

Ensuring an appropriate administrative base for policy implementation may involve the creation of new agencies or sub-units of an existing organization. More usually, however, existing organizations and organizational processes have to be assumed to be appropriate administrative tools. This is one of the major problems. Policy implementation usually involves a process of policy disaggregation: a coherent and explicit policy is broken down into components which are processed through resource, personnel, and other discrete organizational sub-units. The essence of effective implementation is therefore to ensure that the policy survives this period of disaggregation and emerges as a reintegrated whole in the form of appropriate organizational outputs. But administrative processes may well be developed to maintain organizations in working order rather than to implement any one particular policy, and the two are by no means the same thing. Moreover, the organizational structures and processes of government are themselves the object of policies — governance policies — which may or may not be conducive to the successful implementation of any one, specific, policy. A policy of maximum decentralization of decision making, for example, may assist the implementation of a majority of the policies handled by social services departments, but inhibit the implementation of a minority. Put differently, the style of organization may determine the kinds of policies which can be effectively implemented.

Securing an appropriate resource environment is so obviously fundamental to the implementation of policy that it need not be laboured here. The key caveat which we have entered is that in public services the use of resources is again a field of potentially independent policy-making. There can be no presumption that output, or service, policies and resource policies will be compatible one with another unless a political commitment — a meta-policy — is made to subordinate one policy stream to another. In the social services, the seventies was a decade of transition between what now appear to be sharply divergent meta-policies; from a period in which resource policies tended to be subordinated to service policies in general terms to one in which there is an even more clearly annunciated determination to subordinate service policies. What is far less clear is whether the present resource policy is to obtain long-term cost-effectiveness as well as short-term cuts, or whether short-term cuts dominate all other considerations.

What we have been attempting to demonstrate is that policy implementation and the running of government organizations both involve the effective handling of administrative processes as well as structures, but that the processes involved are by no means identical — logically, or in practice. The processes needed to run organizations have to be deeply institutionalized in those organizations and usually become sub-units or departments such as finance, policy planning, capital programming and personnel. The process crucial to implementation has first to be identified at the intellectual level, and ways of using organizational processes to give life to policies have then to be found. For this reason it can be argued that the implementation of policy depends upon institutionalized administrative processes, but that the use made of them has to be assessed afresh for every policy: it cannot simply be assumed that a policy will emerge unscathed from organizational processes which apparently exist to implement it but which inevitably result in its disaggregation. Effective policy implementation may therefore require a much larger intellectual and political input than is generally realised — a fact which at least partly underlies accusations by ex-ministers that civil servants obstruct their policy initiatives.

As we have implied, the first step in policy implementation is to ensure that existing organizational structures and processes are appropriate to the policy. If they are not, the choice lies between creating new ones, adapting those which exist or, as may often be inevitable in government, modifying policy to make it more capable of implementation through existing agencies. Once these basic decisions have been made and a coherent policy is to be implemented through a given administrative system, the following implementation processes are crucial: policy explication and communication; securing appropriate resource inputs; exercising control over the production process; exercising control over production output; securing support and compliance.

Each of these may be the province of an organizational process or sub-unit but, as we have argued, implementation depends upon the use of these institutionalized processes for a particular purpose and the integration of them to ensure the effective 'reaggregation' of the policy in the form of outputs. These logically distinct implementation processes are by no means discrete in practice and the 'cross currents' are precisely one of the major areas of difficulty to be considered. By way of illustration, let us note the ways in which policy explication and communication become enmeshed in the control of inputs, production and outputs.

Policy explication can take two main forms: the specification of policy intent and the specification of the action components of producing the desired outputs. The distinction is roughly that between ends and means. The crucial issue, as it appears to us, is that of obtaining the right balance between these two approaches with each group of actors involved in policy implementation. The specification of policy intent may involve the clarification of guiding philosophies and objectives (e.g., preserving the dignity of old people), the statement of the theoretical base of the policy (e.g., ideas about need, causality and intervention) and the setting of precise, possibly quantified, output targets (e.g., the reduction by 50% of mental confusion among old people arising as a result of social isolation and loneliness). Output targets of this kind are rare, and the level of discussion of the theoretical base of policy varies enormously; much room often exists, therefore, for professional or para-professional groups to impose their own theories on policies regardless of their appropriateness to the original objectives. Policy explication often stops once the 'banner goals' underlying policy have been aired, but these banner goals may offer very limited guidance to implementors and may enable a wide range of outputs to be taken as evidence of satisfactory implementation.

On the other hand, many specific controls are exercised over resource inputs, production processes and organizational, or intermediate, outputs. In the health and personal social services, controls of this kind grew in importance throughout the sixties and seventies as a manifestation of planning and have been apparently dismissed by the present Government as the essence of 'dirigism'. They include: the specification of resource input norms (e.g., x number of home helps per thousand of the elderly population); the specification of production processes (e.g., imposing statutory visiting requirements or case reviews on some types of child care work); and the identification of desired organizational, or intermediate, outputs (e.g., y number of meals to be made available per thousand of the elderly population, or z number of places in attendance centres for mentally handicapped adults per thousand of the population). Quality control is also covered in a variety of ways ranging from the inspection and licensing of private homes for old people or the handicapped, to the altogether more ambiguous but influential monitoring of child care through public enquiries into cases of child abuse and neglect.

Let us now turn to the problem of ensuring compliance and support. Etzioni's three types of compliance strategy remain a valid basis for discussion: the application of *sanctions* for non-compliance; the offering of *incentives;* and the moulding of the *normative* structure within which people operate.[10] Each of these can be applied to the securing of compliance from individual actors, or to the relationship between superordinate and subordinate organizations and sub-units (e.g., central-local government relationships or local office-field office relationships).

The use of sanctions to gain compliance is limited in a 'professionally staffed' local authority service in three ways: by the norms of autonomy surrounding local government and professional practice; by the difficulty of establishing standards against which to identify non-compliance; and by the comparatively narrow range of sanctions which can be deployed. Individuals and organizations can be sanctioned by opprobrium: public enquiries and 'performance leagues' are two examples. In addition, unambiguous service provision minima could potentially be used to give 'bite' to the publication of performance leagues, but this route has been eschewed by central government in the past. On the other hand, the existence of planning guidelines which specify desirable levels of service inputs can and have been used by health authorities as a basis for criticizing low provision by local authorities and for threatening non-collaboration; local authorities are in turn not incapable of reciprocating. The most incisive and rapidly growing use of sanctions, however, is the present Government's threat to withhold grant support from 'overspending' authorities. Hitherto, sanctions for non-compliance have been used sparingly in the personal social services; they are now overt and firmly tied to the implementation of resource policies.

The use of incentives has also changed. Incentives for individual staff members rapidly diminish in volume as services move from expansion to stasis or contraction, though the 'currency' (promotion, secondment, etc.) is enhanced as it becomes more scarce. At the organizational level a similar trend has been operating. During the years of expansion the opportunity for budgetary growth was almost universal, but non-specific. It was difficult for central government to offer local authorities financial incentives to move in particular directions because rate support grant is an unhypothecated rather than a specific grant. Control over capital expenditure provided the primary direct source of incentives — and sanctions.[11] Various forms of quasi-specific grants were the main indirect form of influence on the revenue side (urban aid, inner city schemes, and joint financing), apart from exhortations to heed the priorities of the day signalled in central government circulars and white papers. With the deepening of financial constraints, these quasi-specific grants have become much more significant relative to hard-pressed departmental budgets. Influence at the margin is therefore more cumulatively effective than in times of growth, but the capacity to use such money wisely — or at all — also diminishes as base budgets are depleted. Paradoxically, central government and other agencies controlling quasi-specific grants (e.g., health authorities in relation to local authorities through joint financing and local authorities in relation to voluntary agencies through grant aid and fee for service payments) potentially gain greater influence over beleaguered budgets in a time of stringency — without necessarily being able to use it to effect a change of course.

Normative controls have been dominant in implementing personal social services policies, especially service, or output, policies. They have flowed through the professional channel via training and policy development within professional associations, and through the 'administrative/political' channels (government policy debate, policy development in the political policies and policy discussion in the local authority associations). Normative control is both a more attractive and uncertain option than those noted above. Sanctions and incentives tend inevitably to focus on specific aberrations or developments and influence sections of a policy field rather than perceptions of the whole of it. They can also induce rigidity, rather than flexibility and creativity, among practitioners and policy makers alike. Sanctions can induce 'risk avoidance' rather than better practice (which has, at least partly, been the effect of the 'scandals' in child care); incentives can induce opportunism rather than well-directed development. The weakness of sanctions is seen in the tendency to criticize particular authorities for failing to achieve a specific guideline, say the level of provision for old people's homes, rather than to evaluate their overall strategy towards the elderly.

Normative controls therefore have merits quite apart from their compatibility with notions of autonomy. If the 'assumptive worlds' of policy makers and practitioners can be influenced, desired directions of change may be achieved even in turbulent environments. The key components of these 'assumptive worlds' have already been identified: definitions and perceptions of social problems and solutions.

Important as compliance strategies are, however, we need some ideas about the factors which predispose individuals, or agencies, to comply with a policy. We would identify two: the *salience* of that policy to the core tasks or objectives with which the individual or agency identifies and the *congruence* of the intellectual and ideological base of the policy with the 'assumptive world' of the individual or agency.[12] Policies which are seen as peripheral to core tasks or objectives are likely to arouse little sympathy; they may also arouse little antagonism if they are not too demanding. Policies based on non-congruent values, definitions of problems to be solved and methods to be adopted are likely to arouse resistance. Successful policy implementation is therefore likely to hinge on the interplay of receptivity as identified along these two dimensions on the one hand, and compliance strategies on the other.

The picture of policy implementation which we have been outlining is represented diagrammatically in Figure I. Ignoring the arrows for the moment, the four areas of analysis which we have tried to identify are presented as column headings: policy streams; implementation processes; compliance strategies; and compliance behaviour. To these we have added, in the second column, two broad implementation strategies — direct and indirect. *Direct implementation* involves the explicit specification of

FIGURE I

*POLICY IMPLEMENTATION IN THE PERSONAL SOCIAL SERVICES:
AN INITIAL MODEL*

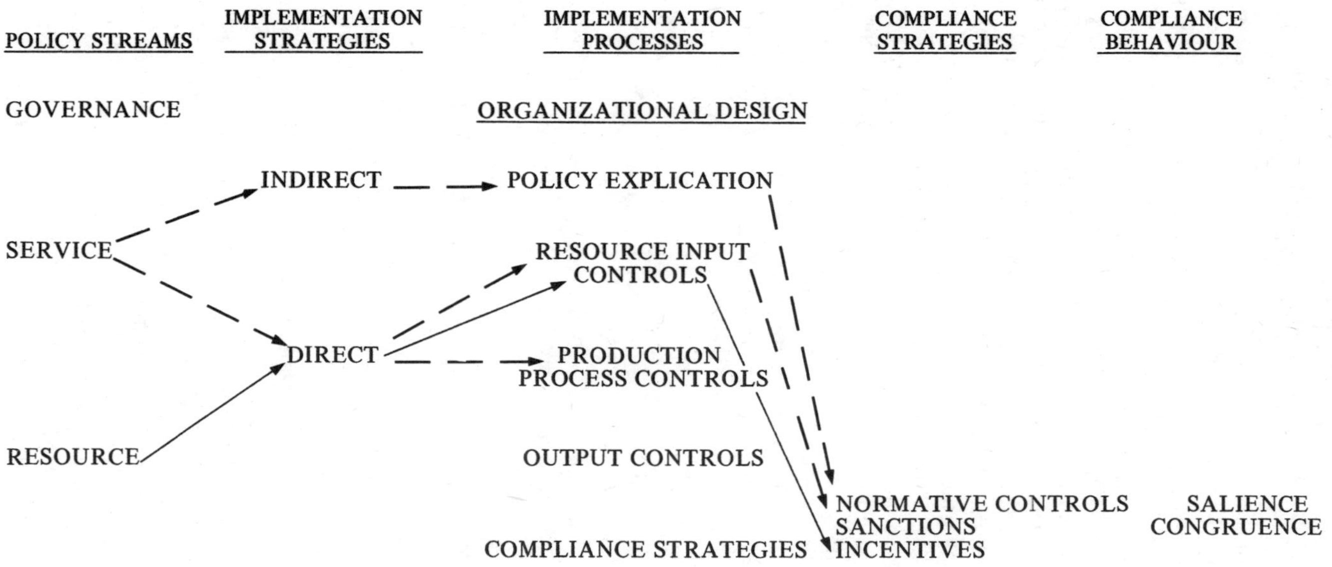

POLICY STREAMS	IMPLEMENTATION STRATEGIES	IMPLEMENTATION PROCESSES	COMPLIANCE STRATEGIES	COMPLIANCE BEHAVIOUR

GOVERNANCE   ORGANIZATIONAL DESIGN

INDIRECT → POLICY EXPLICATION

SERVICE

DIRECT

RESOURCE INPUT CONTROLS

PRODUCTION PROCESS CONTROLS

OUTPUT CONTROLS

RESOURCE

COMPLIANCE STRATEGIES

NORMATIVE CONTROLS
SANCTIONS
INCENTIVES

SALIENCE
CONGRUENCE

desired outputs and/or guidance on the actions, institutions or processes needed to achieve them; it is likely to be supported by explicit incentives or sanctions. *Indirect implementation* involves the creation of a 'climate' within which actors are likely to behave in ways which will achieve desired results. Typically, this means emphasising the ideological or value base of government policy and/or its theoretical and knowledge base.

The arrows in Figure I highlight three of the prominent central government approaches to policy implementation in the personal social services in recent years. The first is the indirect form of service policy implementation through policy explication and normative control. It can be seen at work in policy documents which specify the objectives and philosophy of policy. We have suggested elsewhere, however, that such policy explication has usually remained at or near the level of 'banner goals'.[13] For example, there have only been limited attempts to explain fully what residential care for old people is intended to be about and, as was noted earlier, the same applies to such services as meals on wheels. Much of the 'content' of the indirect channel of policy implementation has frequently derived from the work of academics (e.g., Townsend on residential care)[14] or professional associations, or policy advisory bodies; insofar as 'authoritative' voices of this kind are not disowned by government they can in effect create implicit policies — enshrined in assumptive worlds and the theoretical base of professional practice.

It is noteworthy that post-war Governments have made little attempt to influence the content of professional training, even indirectly. In sum, the indirect approach to policy implementation has been weakly used in general, though quite strongly developed in particular instances (e.g., the work of the National Development Group on the Mentally Handicapped).[15]

The second, direct, approach to implementation also emphasises service policies but it finds expression in the specification of resource inputs — especially in long-term planning — and in some controls exercised over the production process. Examples of the first are the setting of targets for numbers of home helps deployed and the control of capital expenditure. Examples of the second are the requirement that local authorities shall establish a social services committee, the insistence after the Seebohm reorganization that the DHSS should have some influence over the appointment of Directors of Social Services and the specification of statutory visiting in some classes of cases. However, central government has not required local authorities only to employ qualified social workers, for example. No attempts have been made to specify or prescribe final outputs (e.g., levels of loneliness among old people, or juvenile delinquency or non-accidental injury to children).

The third form of implementation concerns the direct translation of resource policies into input targets. The objectives of public expenditure control and cost-effectiveness in service provision have both been pursued in this way, with varying degrees of emphasis and specificity. The general assumption has been that local authorities have autonomy within the limits of the legislative and grants framework set by central government, and expenditure growth restraint targets have not been enforced in a determined way by service area, though overall local authority expenditure levels have been brought under tighter control in the second half of the seventies. Cost-effectiveness guidance has been very general for the most part, with the emphasis on general presumptions about the benefits of community care. Some more precise approaches to cost-effectiveness have been attempted as, for example, in the 'balance of care model' and the quantitative specification by DHSS of priorities between and within services during the early period of expenditure restraint in the mid-seventies.[16] The impact of academic and other commentators, and of local authority innovations, are again an important source of 'implicit policy'. Nevertheless, for all its importance at the rhetorical level, cost effectiveness has not been strongly pursued through direct means, and even expenditure restraint was not backed by heavy sanctions during the seventies. The diagram is therefore by no means an exhaustive summary of implementation strategies. For example, the 'indirect' approach to public expenditure restraint has gradually become overwhelmingly important, such that the intellectual and ideological climate is one in which need and service policy has clearly been swamped at national level by discussion of scarcity. The diagram is merely illustrative of recent styles and channels of policy implementation as a backcloth against which to discuss the present Government's approach.

The crucial feature of these patterns of policy implementation is the apparent gap between the articulation of service policies in terms of generalized banner goals on the one hand and the specification of quantified resource input and intermediate output targets on the other. In fact, there are two gaps: there is little obvious connection between the general and the specific or between service and resource policies. Specific guidelines are rarely linked in a clear way to the theoretical base of policy. As we have seen, it is not clear whether or how a particular level of meals on wheels input could achieve a specific reduction in loneliness or poor nutritional standards among old people. Neither is it clear that any particular mix of home helps, meals on wheels, long-term or short-term residential care or sheltered housing would represent the best value for money or meet a given level of need in the face of expenditure restraint. Consequently, at the planning and the operational levels a range of semi-autonomous bodies of theory and sets of objectives flood in to fill the gap, many of them implicit or vague and generalized if explicit. For example, production processes tend to be based on broad assumptions (or trades union preferences) about the appropriate boundaries of professional and para-professional work and well-entrenched practices such as the almost universal tendency in social work for each 'case' to be handled by one

27

social worker in varying degrees of professional isolation. Similarly, assumptions about what are cost-effective policies and practices (e.g., community care as opposed to care in residential institutions) remain substantially untested. Moreover, the ways in which social workers, home helps or residential care workers actually *use* their time and set about their work is determined more by implicit 'practice theory' about how the job should be done, or rules governing the insurable risks which staff can incur (home helps are not allowed to clean windows), than by the theoretical base of a particular policy or the best use of scarce resources.

These reflections are not intended as a particular criticism of the personal social services, nor of social work. They could be repeated in most areas of social policy. The same lack of detailed follow-through can be seen, for example, in the failure to translate the goals of comprehensive secondary education into proposals for retraining ex-grammar school or secondary modern teachers to teach different types of children.

A major problem of policy implementation is therefore that of bridging the gaps between broad statements of policy and the detailed guidance of production processes and the work of practitioners, and between service, or output, policies and resource policies. The common requirement is what we will call *intermediate theories:* the following through of policy objectives to a level of detail which makes sense as a guideline for practitioners and links them to the strategic concerns of policy. To be successful, such intermediate theories would, in sum, not only spell out service policies for actors at the operational level, but also explore and reconcile service and resource policies for practitioners of all kinds: financial and field staff alike would gain an overall picture of how service and resource objectives might be made compatible.

We are not arguing that this state of policy enlightenment is readily achievable in practice, but merely that it seems to be a crucial need at any level of an organization at which discretion exists if policies are to be implemented successfully. The balance of direct and indirect approaches to implementation is likely to be crucial and has to be compatible with the nature and level of discretionary behaviour which exists or is to be created. We are also, as before, arguing that these logically necessary processes of implementation will not automatically be synonymous with institution-alized organizational processes — which exist for different purposes.

The difference between our view of services based on a balanced approach to policy implementation and services as they usually operate in practice has been well illustrated by the planning of health and personal social services in recent years. Specific guidance, especially on resource input targets and resource allocation priorities, has grown in volume and sophistication, but this guidance has often acted as a *substitute* for policy rather than as a means of policy implementation: service production programming has been dominant. Insofar as it is based on coherent and explicit policies which are so well established as not to need reiteration, programming is a means of implementing policy. The absence of policy, however, can be identified in many areas by asking the question: once resources have been allocated in the recommended ways, how should they actually be *used,* why, and to what effect?

The problem currently, therefore, is as much a problem of having policies to implement — as opposed to organizations to run — as one of inadequate implementation. How can this be? The sixties and seventies were the era of preoccupation with rational planning, programmed budgeting and corporateness; they should surely have produced implementable policies. That they did is clear, but we would argue, as Wildavsky did at the time, that policy analysis became dominated by programme budgeting and, more latterly, service, or output, policies by resource policies.[17] Consequently, the explication of policy and the development of intermediate theory has been relatively ignored in favour of programming service production and controlling resource inputs.

IV Emerging Policies

Using the three policy streams identified earlier, we will now outline the major initiatives taken by the Conservative Government in its first eighteen months of office and discuss the issues of implementation which they raise.

GOVERNANCE POLICIES

The present Government came to office espousing a strongly held and apparently very clear view on the role of the state: that the enlargement of the role of the state and the diminution of the role of the individual and of private enterprise had 'crippled the enterprise and effort on which a prosperous country with improving social services depended;[18] and that the country's relative economic decline could be reversed by the government 'working *with the grain* of human nature, helping people to help themselves — and others.'[19] In the field of health and welfare (as the Manifesto called it), this philosophy has found expression as an intention to limit the role of the state in direct service provision and of central government in the management of local services, whether statutory or non-statutory.

A minimalist approach to central-local relations

The basic approach of DHSS ministers to central-local relations may be characterized as one of 'disengagement',[20] as was illustrated by Patrick Jenkin's response to the criticism levelled at DHSS in 1980 by the House of Commons Social Services Committee:

> Perhaps the most disturbing aspect of this report is its assumption that everything should be managed at Whitehall level and that ministers should preside over every detailed decision. I reject that view. It is the government's firm policy that detailed planning and management of resources are best left to those on the spot who know local needs and priorities.[21]

He argued elsewhere that the growth of the PSS in the 1970s, largely led and promoted by the centre, reflected the dirigiste attitudes of the late 1960s and early 1970s in which emphasis was placed on management, planning and co-ordination . . . but this approach has had costs as well as benefits. There has been some inflexibility and bureaucracy . . . some power of initiative has inevitably been lost to the centre from the community at ground level. This is true both in local communities and between local authorities and central government. . . . The risk is that [centralist thinking] smothers the contribution that the community itself can make.[22]

Few specific initiatives were taken to implement this approach within the PSS. For example, only 4 of the 300 controls listed for repeal in the White Paper 'Central Government Controls over Local Authorities' related to the PSS.[23] The Association of County Councils' suggestion that existing mandatory duties in the PSS should become permissive powers was not accepted. Thus nothing of real consequence to the PSS emerged from that exercise.

Another token of the desire to limit the role of central government — and civil service costs — was the reduction in the number of departmental circulars.[24] However, this may simply have required the local authority associations to communicate with their members more frequently on behalf of central government. A consequence of broader significance was that ministerial speeches became a more important vehicle for the transmission of ministers' views, so much so that some observers characterized 1979 and 1980 as a period of 'government by ministerial speech' in the PSS. It is too early to judge whether the ministerial speech will continue to be a major instrument for the articulation *and* implementation of policy. It is possible that its early dominance simply reflected a temporary policy and administrative vacuum which existed until the department developed programmes and instruments more consistent with its ministers' philosophy of governance. The department's dilemma was how to develop a style of central-local relations which, while eschewing detailed prescriptions on the one hand, did not become one of empty exhortation on the other. The impact of ministerial speeches on local policy makers has not been researched in the PSS and their effectiveness as a tool of implementation is difficult to judge at this stage.

Finally, the Secretary of State has repeatedly emphasised the indicative nature of expenditure White Paper planning figures, reminding local authorities of their freedom to determine priorities between services, providing that they adhered to overall expenditure totals. We discuss this issue further below, noting only at this point the strong feeling in local government circles that the tighter controls on spending in the Local Government Finance (No. 2) Bill sat oddly alongside the declared intention of increased local autonomy.

One question about central-local relations which remained unanswered in 1980 concerned the role left for central government once it had disengaged from the central direction of local action. What, for example, is to be the nature and extent of central involvement in planning and setting priorities and guidelines in the future? A major feature of the 'dirigiste inheritance' is the fairly detailed guidance on priorities and norms for levels of service provision developed in the DHSS, especially in the mid-1970s. This guidance was not abrogated but the philosophy of disengagement made its status ambiguous. A document providing guidance on the implementation of national priorities was promised in 'the autumn' of 1980 but it was not clear what form this would take.[25] The presumption was that less detailed guidance would be introduced, but whether it would be backed up by the reintroduction of a form of centrally co-ordinated planning was less clear. The system of 3-year planning returns (LAPS) inherited by the Government was abandoned in the wake of planned expenditure reductions. We detected some support for its reintroduction in a modified form, but by late 1980 no move had been made in that direction and no new planning guidelines had been issued.

To return to the fundamental question flowing from the stance on central-local relations: precisely what continuing role was envisaged for the Department in the PSS? The answer did not emerge clearly in 1980, though there was a widespread assumption that it would continue to include the formulation of national policies (such as the review of mental handicap policy and the White Paper on the elderly), the raising of resources for the PSS through the PESC system, and the establishment of some kind of national guidance. How those responsibilities could be reconciled with the objective of leaving local decisions to local decision makers remained unclear. The strategic guidance document was expected to provide the first real indication of where, in practice, the balance was to be drawn between local and central responsibilities. Yet, in the event, its publication in February 1981 under the title 'Care in Action' merely underlined the ambiguity of the Department's position. As anticipated, its priorities were broadly in line with those set out by the previous Government. However, they were no longer expressed in financial terms, which raises the question of how progress towards them can be monitored inside or outside government. Moreover, despite wishing to devolve responsibility to local communities, the Secretary of State cannot stand back totally from the PSS. As the Select Committee on Social Services noted in its third report, some form of central government guidance of the personal social services is logically implied in the continued desire to steer the NHS in directions which have direct implications for the PSS.[26]

A reaction against the pre-eminence of statutory services

Ministers in both the DHSS and the Home Office emphasised their commitment to the objective of achieving a new point of balance between statutory and non-statutory welfare systems both before and after coming to office in 1979. Mr. Whitelaw, for example, stated that the Government's 'social policy puts the emphasis of "caring" where it belongs — in society itself.'[27] At the same time, he regretted 'the many forces in the modern world [which] have contributed to an erosion of the sense of local belonging and individual responsibility.'[28] In February 1980, Patrick Jenkin was in no doubt as to the identity of at least one such 'force':

> Is it not clear that over the last two decades we have tended to get the perspective wrong? There has been a tendency to believe that as the statutory services grow, as more and more services are provided by public authorities, so the community can safely entrust their cares and concerns for the elderly, the handicapped and others in need to Town Hall and Whitehall and need not themselves bother overmuch.[29]

While recognizing that statutory services had a key role to play, he argued that:

> They are not and never can be the sole providers of care. Each and every one of us has a personal responsibility to the community in which we live and it is through our families, through our neighbourhoods, through the voluntary bodies in all their manifestations that we can best express that responsibility.[30]

Consequently, as he told the PSS Conference in November 1980, 'A greater encouragement of voluntary and community effort will now be a central thrust of our policy towards the PSS.'[31] In principle, greater encouragement of the private sector might also have been expected but little was apparent, especially in comparison with ministerial rhetoric and action in respect of private health care.

RESOURCE POLICIES

Two main objectives — the constraint of public expenditure and the pursuit of cost-effectiveness — may be discerned within the Government's resource policies. The former dominated the latter and arguably made its achievement more difficult. Indeed, expenditure control appeared to take precedence over initiatives in all policy streams: there was no lack of central intervention in attempts to restrict the *overall* level of public expenditure. In this section, we identify resource policy as developed in 1979 and 1980 and review its implementation in relation to both the patterns and levels of expenditure set out in Government guidance to the PSS. We also consider the relationship between the implementation of expenditure control and cost-effectiveness policies.

The policy framework: the personal social services and the economy

The national economic situation and the Government's economic policy invariably formed the framework within which the Secretary of State discussed his approach to the PSS. He repeatedly referred to the 'over-riding economic imperative'. When challenged about the primacy of economic policy (particularly as reflected in public expenditure policy), his response was to deny that expenditure had been pruned without regard for its social consequences:

> Far from undermining the social services we are in fact pursuing the only policy which would have any hope of safeguards for the future.[32]

This approach was quite consistent with the Government's view that the restoration of the country's economic health was, inter alia, dependent on a reduction both of taxation and the Public Sector Borrowing Require-ment (PSBR). Nonetheless, it raised questions about the extent to which the nature of the PSS and the demands placed upon them were, at least initially, understood by this Government. It may be argued that the workload of the PSS is related to economic factors in much the same way as is demand for social security benefits. Unemployment is associated with a high incidence of mental illness and family breakdown; it also reduces the employment opportunities of those 'marginal' workers who are concen-trated within the clientele of the PSS.[33] There is a case, therefore, for budgeting for the consequent increased pressures on PSS in much the same way that projected increases in unemployment benefit claims are fed into the social security programme. Patrick Jenkin's response was to accept that 'in an ideal world' there would be a case for expanding the PSS in such circumstances 'but in a time of low economic growth there is an absence of resources . . . it is no use having a bleeding heart if you haven't got the money to pay for it.'[34]

Expenditure plans within the personal social services

The Government's objectives towards the overall level of public expenditure were, first, to 'stabilize' expenditure at 1978/79 levels and then to reduce it progressively. Various commitments and priorities had to be accommodated within the overall expenditure targets. These included commitments to increase spending on defence and law and order and to maintain the planned levels of expentiture on the NHS. Some level of increase in social security expenditure was accepted as inevitable. Local government expenditure was therefore a prominent target area for cuts. Planned expenditure in that sector in 1980/81 was to be 3.1% less than in 1978/79, compared with an *increase* of 3.1% in central government spending. Given this context, how did the PSS fare in the Government's spending plans?

There were three phases of public expenditure review up to the end of 1980, separately covering the financial years 1979/80; 1980/81; and 1981/82 to 1983/84.

Fiscal year 1979/80. Public authorities were already more than two months into the new financial year when, in his June 1979 Budget, the Chancellor announced the objective of holding total expenditure for 1979/80 at the 1978/79 level. To this end, local authorities were expected to reduce current expenditure by 3% (£360m) and were informed that the Rate Support Grant Increase Order due in November 1979 would not fully reflect the effect of pay settlements to the extent of at least £300m. DOE circular 21/79 (7 July 1979) included the following *guidance on effecting savings:* 'It is, of course, for each authority to decide, in the light of its own needs and priorities, within and between services how to achieve these savings. However, authorities will be aware of the Government's wish to give priority to law and order services.'[35] The Chancellor's Budget statement had also expressed the hope that the 'most vulnerable' would be protected from the consequences of expenditure reductions.

Expenditure plans: 1980/81: A White Paper,[36] unique in covering just one year's expenditure (1980/81), was published in November 1979. This confirmed that further reductions in local authority spending were required: 4.5% less than the expected out-turn for 1979/80 based on plans in the preceding Government's White Paper (plans superseded by the June Budget Statement), or 3.1% less than the 1978/79 provisional out-turn.

The White Paper assumed a distribution of current expenditure between local authority services which reflected its 'view of national priorities between and within services in 1980/81'.[37] However, it accepted that such figures were 'necessarily tentative since it is for individual local authorities to decide the eventual distribution in the light of local needs and conditions'.[38] Nonetheless, for the PSS the assumed distribution of current expenditure indicated a *reduction in spending greater than that for the local authority sector as a whole:*

compared with the provisional out-turn for 1978/79 the figure was 4.7%;
compared with the expected out-turn for 1979/80 (based on the Labour Government's plans for that year) the figure was 6.7%;
compared with the Labour Government's plans for 1980/81 it was 8.9%.

Large though such figures might appear, they under-represented the full magnitude of the reduction in expenditure proposed for the PSS: previous White Papers had accepted that merely to maintain levels of services a *growth* rate of 2% p.a. was necessary to take account of growing numbers of the elderly and children in care. Moreover, the adequacy of this proposed growth rate had been contested in the past, on the grounds that it was insufficient to cover other factors such as increased unit costs and the revenue consequences of previous years' capital programmes.[39] In such circumstances, the treatment of education — the largest consumer of local authority resources — only served to emphasise the disproportionate impact on the PSS of the search for savings in public expenditure. The 6.7% reduction on the 1979/80 expected out-turn for the PSS contrasted with one of 4.8% for education, even though that service faced *reduced* client demand in some sectors of its work.

The guidance to local authorities on how savings might be effected included:[40] 'further increases in efficiency'; the development of 'policies designed to help people help themselves'; and the promotion of 'collaboration with the voluntary sector'. Where reduced standards of provision proved necessary, authorities were exhorted to 'protect the most vulnerable' and 'to give as far as possible priority to those services for children which are concerned with the prevention and treatment on what constitute the 'most vulnerable groups' *within* the PSS. In practice, that would have presented a task of extreme difficulty. As we have indicated above, the PSS may legitimately be regarded as the local government service in which responsibilities for the 'most vulnerable' are explicitly concentrated.

Expenditure plans: 1981/82 — 1983/84: The results of the Government's first full survey of public expenditure were published in a White Paper in March 1980.[41] Local authority current expenditure was planned to fall by 4% and capital expenditure by 14%, in real terms, between 1979/80 and 1983/84. However, in contrast with the disproportionately large cuts indicated for 1980/81, *real growth* was now indicated for the PSS. The amounts — 2% in 1981/82, 2.3% in 1982/83 and 1.5% in 1983/84 — left the PSS considerably below the Labour Government's planned expenditure for those years, but restored them to approximately the level of planned expenditure inherited for 1979/80. Patrick Jenkin announced that this element of growth should be sufficient to maintain standards given the increase in numbers of the elderly and of children in care.[42] However, this would represent, of course, the maintenance of *reduced* standards if the 1980/81 cuts were implemented.

An increase in resources available to the PSS in 1980/81 was also announced at the same time in the shape of a 16% real increase in the Joint Finance programme. This programme makes funds available from NHS resources to finance PSS schemes which can be represented as benefiting the health service. The total increase — to which ministers gave particular emphasis in defending their expenditure policies — amounted to less than 10% of the planned reduction in PSS spending for 1980/81, which underlines an apparent divergence between different elements of the

Department's resource policies. However, because the amounts allocated to individual projects are withdrawn progressively, normally over five or seven-year periods, any increase in the Joint Finance programme is a two-edged sword: local authorities have gradually to take full financial responsibility for projects in future years.

Despite the resumption of demographically related growth and the enhancement of Joint Finance allocations, at the end of 1980 the PSS faced the prospect of meeting increased demand from a lower resource base than was originally planned, assuming the new expenditure levels were achieved. To that extent, the reduction in spending indicated for 1980/81 represented a fundamental change in resource policy (as Gerard Vaughan initially conceded to the Select Committee) and not merely a temporary disruption of previous policies (as he subsequently sought to argue).[43] By imposing a sharp expenditure reduction in one year and subsequently restoring a limited rate of growth, the long-term 'expenditure profile' had been lowered without the necessity for a continuing series of cuts. Nevertheless, these were only planned expenditures and the outcome depended upon local government reactions.

The personal social services and cost-effectiveness

Resource policies need not concentrate solely on the expansion or compression of public expenditure; they may extend to the pattern of resource utilization. Three notions of cost-effective development surfaced in the first eighteen months of the Government's life: the reduction of 'unproductive bureaucracy', including central government control and guidance of local authorities; the shift to the voluntary sector; and the movement from residential to community care.[44] In addition, resource restraint was presented as an opportunity to search creatively for improved resource utilization.[45] In recent decades cost-effectiveness has been pursued in two rather different ways in the 'health and welfare' services. A sophisticated body of analytical techniques (cost-benefit, cost-effectiveness, production function and output analyses) have slowly been applied, experimentally, to these services. At the same time, a far less sophisticated and generalized preference for 'community care' has been advanced — not least on the grounds of the presumed economy and cost-effectiveness of this approach. The same broad strategy has also been advocated on purely service policy considerations of need and client preference.

However, the 'community care policy' has come to embrace potentially conflictual emphases:

(a) shifting the burden of social care from health to social services;

(b)   shifting the care burden from institutional to 'in the community' services (e.g., from residential to day and domiciliary services) in both health and social services;

(c)   shifting the care burden from statutory to non-statutory provision, while concentrating statutory services on those with no, or only inadequate, sources of non-statutory care;

(d)   identifying priorities between different client groups in recognition of the pressure on public services and the legacy of differential neglect of the key client groups.

There is little evidence of these public policies having been based on closely analytical, as opposed to 'common sense', notions of what is cost-effective. Indeed, there is only a limited body of cost-effectiveness research on which policy could have been based — some of it supporting and some challenging the underlying assumptions of the 'common sense' view. The Department has had to acknowledge that it is 'particularly difficult to draw firm conclusions' from much of the completed research, but it has undertaken to take into account what evidence is available in considering the balance between health and PSS spending and in preparing strategic guidance.[46]

Nevertheless, it is clear that the Government inherited a body of resource utilization policies of varying degrees of specificity and sophistication. It also inherited the paradox that moving the care burden from the health to the social services ((a) above) can well involve *increased,* not decreased, expenditure on residential provision in local authorities ((b) above). Such a course certainly involves *increased capital expenditure* by local authorities, which cuts across one of the simplest and 'least painful' approaches to overall resource restraint. In itself, this problem is merely a particular example of the fact that different resource policies are not necessarily mutually reinforcing. Most fundamentally, anything less than a steady rate of growth somewhat above the 2% level calculated as necessary to meet demand pressure would mean that a switch from health to social services could not be effected even with the assistance of joint finance monies — or that these desiderata could only be achieved at the expense of existing clients and areas of work.

The present Government's inheritance was therefore deeply paradoxical — purely in resource policy terms. Indeed, it can be argued that the levels of funding provided by the Labour Government represented an abandonment of community care as a policy. Given its predilections, the new Government was faced with the alternatives of maintaining or increasing PSS expenditure in support of the community care policy as a cost-effective strategy; abandoning this policy — at least temporarily — in favour of expenditure cuts; or combining either of these approaches with a more detailed and thorough questioning of cost-effectiveness.

In the event, the inherited paradoxes have been enriched by the general defence of the voluntary sector (partly on cost-effectiveness grounds) and by the adoption of a policy of differentially heavy cuts followed by one of minimal (demographically, barely adequate) planned growth. By late 1980 it was perhaps more uncertain than ever before whether 'community care' meant anything in practice, though Sir George Young's advocacy of resource transfer mechanisms suggested that the inter-dependence of resource and service policies might secure some form of practical recognition. In fact, Patrick Jenkin did accept that his spending policies implied some 'adverse effect' on community care policies and that it might 'indeed prove difficult to avoid retreating a little'.[47] Subsequently, the Select Committee has recommended that the DHSS give high priority to research on the cost-effectiveness of different packages of care.[48] However, there remained the complication that the reigning philosophy of governance could preclude, or severely hamper, the translation of research lessons into firm central guidance.

The implementation of expenditure policy

During the period covered by this monograph, discussion of expenditure policy centred around an ill-defined concept of expenditure 'cuts'. The impossibility of making the planned level of expenditure reductions without also cutting direct services to clients was also emphasised. Several surveys, of varying degrees of coverage and sophistication, were mounted to demonstrate the scale and nature of the 'cuts'.[49] The surveys conducted by the Personal Social Services Council (PSSC) and by the Association of Directors of Social Services (ADSS), reported findings of cuts both in spending and in services provided. The ADSS survey for example, reported cuts in expenditure of 2.5% in 1979/80 within a range of 0.05% to 7.7%.[50] The PSSC findings were similar: 'the average reduction in expenditure expected of social service departments for 1979/80 may be between 2½ and 3%, concealing a range stretching from 0.5% to 8%.'[51] For his part, the Secretary of State recognized that spending reductions in real terms implied the need for local authorities to face 'agonising decisions',[52] though he also affirmed his belief that the situation on the ground was less serious than 'the more hysterial journals seek to make out'.[53] Indeed, his reaction to the surveys' findings and the criticisms which they evoked was essentially unapologetic. While emphasising the indicative nature of White Paper planning figures for individual services, he nonetheless asserted that the level of savings required could be achieved by rooting out inefficiency and unproductive bureaucratic waste without significantly affecting the quality or quantity of services. He also argued that expenditure constraint acted as an incentive to more imaginative and cost-effective ways of caring. The ADSS took a very different view, arguing that it was impossible to achieve the desired savings by reducing growth alone or by limiting them to administrative and clerical costs and to 'good housekeeping' measures. It concluded that, 'there can be no doubting the fact that actual services to clients have been reduced and in some cases quite seriously affected.'[54] The final report by the staff of the PSSC came to a similar conclusion about the effects of expenditure policy in levels of services: 'Hopes that public expenditure cuts could be made solely from cutting administrative waste have proved illusory. Reductions in direct services to consumers have been necessary in order to make the required savings.'[55]

'Cuts' or 'growth in 1979/80 and 1980/81? Given the agreement on all sides that 'cuts' in PSS expenditure *were* taking place, together with a considerable amount of 'evidence' providing examples of their effects on the ground, many were surprised to discover that, in practice, the PSS continued to experience expenditure growth in constant price terms. In July 1980 the Consultative Council on Local Government Finance was presented with estimated out-turn figures for 1979/80 showing that spending on the PSS had not only been increased, rather than reduced, but that expenditure was 1.4% greater than had been allowed for in the previous Labour Government's RSG settlement for that year.[56] Further growth in SSD expenditure was also being planned by local authorities for 1980/81. Social services departments' original budgets for 1980/81 were, according to returns made to the DOE, 14% above the White Paper's figure (which indicated that a 6.7% cut should take place). As overall spending by local authorities was 5.6% above government targets, the Environment Secretary required them to submit revised budgets. These showed local authority spending to be 2.6% above target and led him to respond by withholding £200m from the RSG increase order and to 'penalize' fourteen 'high-spending' authorities. The revised budgets showed SSDs to be some 12% above the White Paper's figure, or 5% above the 1978/79 out-turn and 2% above the 1979/80 expected out-turn.[57]

Nonetheless, it would be a mistake to conclude from this evidence of expenditure growth in 1979/80 and 1980/81 that there were no 'cuts' in the PSS during those years. How is this apparent contradiction to be explained? Is it possible to reconcile the two quite different pictures with which we have been presented of the local impact of the Government's resource policy? A partial explanation is that the ADSS figure of a 2.5% cut related to the budgets of only 62 authorities out of 120 surveyed throughout the United Kingdom. The DOE figures covered the whole of England. Significantly, 16 of the 78 authorities who responded to ADSS made no cuts at all, and thus the 2.5% figure could have been an over-statement of the situation nationally. As a further example of the incomplete nature of the data on which the discussion of 'cuts' took place in 1979 and 1980, the ADSS survey found that 37 establishments

41

were to be closed in 1979/80, with 51 other closures planned for 1980/81 (the majority in both years being children's establishments). The corresponding figures for delayed openings of new establishments were 31 and 35 respectively.[58] Yet, information was not obtained on the number of new establishments opened during 1979/80 or scheduled to be opened during 1980/81. Indeed, and this is illustrative of how the debate on resource policy implementation was structured totally in terms of 'cuts', the ADSS survey did not seek information about increases or growth in budgets,[59] though some directors did provide it. It was not disputed that some new capital projects were commissioned in 1979/80, but it was not possible to say how many, nor whether they were made possible only by making reductions elsewhere in the base budget.

A second and more significant explanation for the divergence between DOE and ADSS statistics is that they did not employ the same *base-lines:* the DOE 1979/80 figures compared *out-turns* with the RSG and expenditure White Paper guidelines while ADSS compared final and original budget *estimates.* Where authorities' original budgets for 1979/80 exceeded the Labour Government's guidelines, 2-3% cuts, however painfully achieved, could still leave them spending more in real terms in 1979/80 than in 1978/79.

What is a 'cut'?   This raises a fascinating question: when is a cut not a cut? Is it really possible to speak of cuts having been made even though real growth in expenditure has taken place? To answer such questions it is necessary to develop a typology of cuts — however crude and provisional.

The only feasible way of disentangling the conceptual confusion surrounding the term 'cuts' is to specify the simplest sort of circumstances in which no cut could be said to have taken place. Having identified what is *not* a cut, we will be better able to note different notions of what *is* a cut. Service provision in one year would represent a 'standstill' compared with the previous year in the following cases:

(a)   a constant volume of services of a standard quality is provided;

(b)   any changes (purely local changes, or national changes reflected locally) in the cost of providing a standard quality of service are fully reflected as increases or decreases in the budget;

(c)   need remains constant;

(d)   services are provided free or at a charge which remains constant relative to other price changes;

(e)   no non-financial constraints (such as controls over manpower) affect the production of a constant volume of a standard quality of service.

42

Some of the principal complications which arise can now be readily perceived. A constant volume of service may be provided against a backcloth of increasing or decreasing need. Changes in service quality may occur which necessitate changes in budget, or service volume, or both. Local changes in the costs of production may not be fully reflected in budgets, especially where the budgets are nationally negotiated. New projects developed in the previous year create resource implications for future years which may not be accurately reflected in the budget and charges made to the public may also change relative to other prices. Bearing these factors in mind, several important types of cut may be noted as follows.

(i) *Cuts in growth* — the growth increment may be reduced or eliminated leaving the base budget untouched. This is *not* a cut in the sense identified above unless the growth is entirely justified by increases in need, but the practice of planning for growth ensures that it is *experienced* as a cut.

(ii) *Cuts in 'service volume' and 'service quality'* — where insufficient allocations have been made to cover inflation (e.g., in cash limits), the full effects of pay and price increases can be met by reductions in service volume. This so called 'volume squeeze' more than fully absorbed the NHS 'growth' allocation (of £86m) for 1979-80, leaving a 'net cut' over the previous year of £56m.[60] Comparable figures are not available for the PSS, but pay awards to social workers and residential staff were well in excess of the cash limits. It is, therefore, highly probable that the 'purchasing power' of any real growth in PSS expenditure during 1980/81 was undermined by these and other increases in unit costs. There may, of course, be opportunities for trading reductions in the quality of service against reductions in volume by substituting cheaper resources such as less well qualified staff, but such changes may take longer to effect.

(iii) *Cuts in the base budget* — this is apparently self-explanatory and would arise from (ii) above. However, even when the real value of the previous year's expenditure is maintained, cuts in the base budget and therefore in the volume of services provided during the previous year may be necessary in order to accommodate the consequences of, for example, Joint Finance commitments, the full year effect of new schemes begun during the previous year and the revenue consequences of capital schemes to be opened during the coming year.

(iv) *Cuts in 'service cover'* — where resource growth does not match growth in need or demand, the same level of service can no longer be provided to the same porportion of a given client group. This is a constant problem in personal social services budgeting in view of the inexorable growth in the numbers of the very elderly.

(v) *Cuts in gross budgets* — the Government has encouraged local authorities to maintain levels of service by increasing charges. Some commentators have described charges (especially where the increase is greater than the rate of inflation) as 'cuts', even though it is not intended that the volume of service provided should be reduced. One justification for so describing them is that increased charges reduce the redistributive effect of the PSS; another is that they may act as a deterrent — reducing demand in the short term and, more speculatively, increasing demand for possibly more expensive services in the longer term. ADSS found that 60 out of the 78 authorities which responded to its survey had increased charges or introduced new ones.[61]

Expenditure outcomes in 1979/80 and 1980/81. Comprehensive information about levels of expenditure and provision is not yet available for the financial years 1979/80 and 1980/81. Consequently it is not fully possible to apply data to our typology of cuts to identify the impact of expenditure decisions taken during the whole of the Government's first eighteen months in office. However, sufficient material exists to show that, taking the country as a whole, many of the fears for the future of the PSS were greatly exaggerated, at least in respect of 1979/80. It is now clear that local authority decisions ensured that the PSS continued to secure preferential treatment during that year compared with total public expenditure and the local authority sector as a whole. Figures supplied to the Select Committee on Social Services confirm an increase rather than a decrease in spending on the PSS during 1979/80. For England as a whole the increase in net current expenditure, at constant prices, was 4.4%.[62] Even more surprisingly, perhaps, in view of the nature of the concern about the 'cuts' in PSS expenditure, this growth of 4.4% was actually greater than that achieved in any of the final three years of the previous administration. Year-on-year growth rates in current expenditure for that period were: 2.8% (1976/77); 1.7% (1977/78); and 4.1% (1978/79).[63]

It must be stressed, however, that national aggregate data mask considerable variations both between different types of local authority and within each category of authority. County councils experienced a lower rate of growth (3%) than metropolitan districts (5.0%), while increases in expenditure were even higher in outer and inner London boroughs (5.7% and 6.4% respectively).[64]

Similarly, the experience of individual social services departments varied substantially: 10 (of 108) were shown in the Select Committee's report as having lower levels of expenditure during 1979/80 than in 1978/79. The size of these reductions ranged from 6.7% to 0.1%. Thus, slightly less than 10% of English departments did experience *absolute* cuts in levels of spending during 1979/80. In addition, the level of growth in a further 15 authorities was less than 2%. Thus a total of 25 authorities (23%) failed to secure the level of growth calculated nationally to be necessary for the maintenance of existing levels of provision for growing client populations.

Nonetheless, the fact remains that for the most part, the 'cuts' about which the PSS community was so greatly exercised took the form in 1979/80 of *cuts in growth rather than cuts in base budgets*. Even so, cuts in existing services might still have been necessary, either to free resources for previously planned developments and other commitments or to meet the effects of a 'volume squeeze'. The existence of local variations in spending should not be overlooked either, since they would appear to imply an absolute reduction in levels of services provided to some communities and, in others, a reduction of levels of service cover proportionate to the growing client populations served. However, it would be unwise to assume too direct a relationship between changes in levels of net expenditure and changes in levels of services provided — and still less changes in levels of welfare experienced by individuals. Expenditure policy is an area in which the uncertainties of implementation are manifold both in relation to the extent to which White Paper spending 'plans' are actually enacted and the consequences of such acts of commission or omission. Discounting, but only for the purposes of this discussion, the issue of policy impacts, we may assume that what really matters to clients is the availability of services. In practice this reflects the skill with which resource and service policies are reconciled locally and not merely the pattern of local expenditure decisions. It is important to note, therefore, that the *use* of resources may produce a pattern of local variation in service outputs different from the pattern of resource inputs.

This addition of a service *outputs* dimension to our discussion of expenditure cuts is important because it takes us beyond the narrow preoccupation with changes in levels of expenditure (which has characterized much of the debate so far on 'the cuts') and prompts us to ask what such changes actually mean in terms of services for clients in local communities. For example, since the Select Committee's data are for net expenditure, some of the reductions shown could be accounted for simply by real increases in charges and/or the utilization of joint finance to 'subsidize' departmental budgets while levels and patterns of service production remain unchanged. Alternatively, improved efficiency, a shift to more cost-effective patterns of care and the substitution of non-statutory for statutory services could all, in principle, produce budgetary savings without necessarily leading to reductions in levels or standards of services delivered to clients — though they might equally have less benign consequences. The point is that we require a much more detailed analysis at the level of individual departments before we can assess with any confidence the impact of the present Government's expenditure decisions on the services provided by the PSS during 1979/80.

The extent to which charges for services have been increased is another aspect of expenditure policy implementation for which further information is required. Although increases in charges for day and domiciliary services were highlighted as a device employed by considerable numbers of

SSDs in their search for savings, it is doubtful whether their overall contribution was very significant. Some indication of the general position may be gained from a comparison of net expenditures as a proportion of gross expenditures in the years 1978/79 and 1979/80. Little change is shown by such comparisons: according to the CIPFA PSS Actuals, total net expenditure in all authorities represented 81.9% of total gross expenditure in 1978/79 and 82.5% in 1979/80.[65] The evidence in relation to individual activities does not all point in the same direction: income was, for example, a higher proportion of gross expenditure on day centres and clubs (except those for the mentally ill), home helps, and meals. Yet it was a lower proportion of spending on Adult Training Centres and day care for the mentally ill. It was rare for any such increases or decreases to exceed 1% of gross expenditure. Moreover, it must be remembered that income is derived from specific grants and joint finance as well as from fees and charges. There is thus no necessary relationship between changes in the proportion of net to gross expenditure and increases in charges. The home help service is the only one for which data on charges are explicitly provided. These show income from charges to be only a slightly higher proportion (0.3%) of gross expenditure in 1979/80 than 1978/79.

In summary, therefore, it appears unlikely that increases in charges were a very significant feature of expenditure policy in the PSS as a whole. This is not to say, of course, that this may not have been the case in relation to individual services in individual departments. Equally, relatively small increases in income from charges in relation to total expenditure might represent substantial increases in charges themselves. Once again, however, there are too many uncertainties surrounding the evidence currently available to permit firm conclusions to be drawn.

Changes in levels of service outputs. Some measure of what the 4.4% growth in net expenditure meant for changes in levels of service outputs may be gained from Table I, derived from the CIPFA Personal Social Services Actuals for 1979/80. It should be noted that CIPFA counsels caution in making year-to-year comparisons from its series. One limiting factor is that there are small changes in the number of authorities covered each year: in 1978/79 113 out of 116 authorities made returns compared with 112 in 1979/80. Nonetheless, while we accept the probability of error in its fine detail, we can be confident that Table I constitutes a tolerably accurate representation of the direction of change in levels of provision during 1979/80.

The picture which emerges presents a considerable, indeed striking, contrast to that contained in the surveys of 'cuts'. Taking England and Wales as a whole, the pattern is one of extension to a number of services combined with reductions in others — most notably residential services for children and the elderly (the figures for aids, adaptations and telephones are of limited significance since they represent less than 1% of

TABLE I

LEVELS OF SERVICE PROVISION 1975/76–1979/80 (ENGLAND AND WALES)

	000s	INDICES OF CHANGE					% CHANGE 1979/80 ON 1978/79
	1975/76	1975/76	1976/77	1977/78	1978/79	1979/80	
RESIDENTIAL CARE							
Elderly	120.3	100	104	105.5	104.8	104.1	(−0.7)
Children	37.3	100	100	97.3	91.7	90.5	(−1.2)
Mentally ill	3.6	100	116.6	127.7	127.7	135.3	(+7.6)
Mentally handicapped adults	9.1	100	112.1	124.2	128.6	138.5	(+9.9)
Mentally handicapped children	1.8	100	105.5	116.6	116.6	122.1	(+5.5)
Physically handicapped	6.0	100	110	115	121.7	123.6	(+1.9)
'COMMUNITY CARE'							
Home helps							
Number (WTE)	50.1	100	93.0	97.2	99.2	96.9	(−2.3)
Cases	670.5	100	102.9	107.8	109.2	113.6	(+4.4)
Hours service	80,622.3	100	99.9	101.7	102.8	104.3	(+1.5)
Hours service per case	120.3	100	97.0	95.3	93.0	90.5	(−2.7)
Meals	41,276.0	100	100.2	99.4	97.5	103.9	(+5.9)
Telephones							
No. of installations assisted	15.1	100	76.2	97.4	118.5	97.8	(−20.7)
No. of rentals assisted	70.0	100	105.1	118	122.6	137.7	(+15.1)
Aids	240.5	100	100.4	114.2	120.5	115.4	(−5.1)
Adaptations	50.3	100	108.3	114.7	135.2	114.1	(−21.1)
Holidays	101.2	100	86.2	85.3	88.6	89.3	(+0.7)
No. of sheltered housing units assisted	90.4	100	103.2	101	83.3	86.0	(+3.6)
Children boarded out	31.8	100	106.9	110.4	111.6	116.2	(+4.6)
Fieldwork staff	21.0	100	105.7	109.5	114.3	119.7	(+5.4)
Administrative staff	17.2	100	109.3	114.5	109.3	107.2	(−2.1)

SOURCE: CIPFA, 'Personal Social Services Statistics: Actuals' 1975/76, 1976/77, 1977/78, 1978/79 and 1979/80.

NOTE: Number of authorities covered (maximum 116):   1975/76 = 111;   1976/77 = 112;   1977/78 = 113;   1978/79 = 113;   1979/80 = 112.

total net expenditure). Taken together, it is tempting to describe the picture as one of growth for the 'minor' client groups (mentally ill, mentally handicapped and physically handicapped) and of 'substitution' for the major client groups (elderly and children).

The 'evidence' for substitution takes the form of reductions in the numbers receiving residential care in both groups combined with, in the case of children, increases in the numbers of fieldworkers and of children boarded out, and, in the case of the elderly, increases in home help cases, home help hours, meals served at home, and units of sheltered housing supported. We would be cautious about drawing such a conclusion too categorically, however. The CIPFA data, for example, provide little useful information on day care, which makes it impossible to gain a clear picture of change in total service packages offered to most client groups with the exception of children and the mentally handicapped where some evidence is available. In addition, an apparently rational pattern of service outputs at the national level may simply be the aggregate of far less rational patterns at the level of individual departments. There is some additional evidence, however, of departments explicitly substituting alternative patterns of care for residential services in the case of children.[66]

Whether this is also true of the elderly is more doubtful since some authorities were reported[67] to be reducing both residential and community care services for that group, and the evidence on changes in residential care is ambiguous.[68] Even where authorities have explicitly switched resources from residential to community care for the elderly, the appropriateness of such an approach is open to doubt, especially from a perspective which spans both the health and PSS. The rapidly growing numbers of very frail and of mentally infirm elderly persons impose limitations on the extent to which such a switch in resources is possible without simply adding to the demand for 'residential care' in the NHS.

Moreover, it is by no means apparent that resources are being increased on a scale sufficient to meet the intensification of need implied by rising numbers and levels of disability. The reduced number of home help hours provided per case (-2.7%) suggests the possibility that, in practice, domiciliary support is being more thinly spread among a more dependent population. On the other hand, it is also possible that any such dilution in service cover is being offset by the growth in day care and domiciliary nursing services which, during the life-time of the previous administration, exceeded the rate of growth in the numbers of persons over 65 and over 75 years of age. The number of local authority day care places, for example, increased by nearly 32% between 1975 and 1978. It should also be noted that the provision, on average, of fewer home help hours per recipient of service represents the continuation of a trend evident during the years of Labour Government: hours provided per case were 15.2% fewer in 1978/79 than in 1974/75. Indeed, apart from the absence of wholesale reductions in service levels, perhaps the most significant aspect of the 1979/80 data is the degree of *continuity* which exists between it and trends in service development under the previous administration.

As Table I demonstrates, both the growth of provision for the 'minor' client groups and the substitution of non-residential for residential patterns of care for children were well established under the Labour Government. Residential care for the elderly decreased in 1978/79 as well as 1979/80, as did the number of administrative staff. Trends in the provision of home help services were also similar in previous years to that experienced in 1979/80, though the increase in the provision of meals is actually against the trend of the previous two years. It may be argued that such continuity is only to be expected: the original expenditure and service plans for 1979/80 were, after all, laid while the previous Government was still in office and in relation to its RSG settlement and guidance on priorities. This would, however, serve to emphasise the slightness of the present Government's impact upon spending and service patterns during 1979/80. It also highlights the need to monitor closely any variations in trends as they emerge for 1980/81 and subsequent years.

There is a further point of interest which emerges from the comparison of change in residential services: residential care consumed precisely the same proportion (47.3%) of gross expenditures on PSS in 1979/80 as in 1978/79. The number of persons in residential care was also all but identical in the two years, there being an increase of under 0.1% in 1979/80. At first sight this suggests a pattern of incremental budgeting. Yet, as we have seen, the reality — nationally — was one of growth in residential services for some client groups and reductions for others, a salutary example of the possibility that decisional outputs which appear incremental at one level of analysis may appear 'rational' at another. In this case, the differential patterns of change between client groups may be represented as illustrative of the ambiguity surrounding the concept of 'community care': in the case of children and the elderly the broad thrust of national policy has been towards an interpretation of the term as 'non-institutional', while in respect of the mentally ill and handicapped the connotation has more often been 'non-hospital'. We would also emphasise that the rationality or otherwise exhibited by patterns of service outputs are not necessarily indicative of a rational *process* of decision making at work. Indeed, the requirement to make cuts, albeit cuts in growth, part way through a financial year is unlikely to promote rational analysis in relation to service policy objectives. The primary criteria by which immediate savings can be identified are, by definition, the speed and facility by which they can be effected (perhaps tempered by their political acceptability) rather than their contribution to policy objectives — or to cost-effectiveness.

We have indicated the speculative nature of some of these comments and have noted the limitations of the data on which our comparisons have been made. Yet, there can be no doubt that the reality of 1979/80 was far from that somewhat balefully predicted: there is no evidence of the dismemberment of the PSS, taking England and Wales as a whole, though this is not to say that the situation in a small minority of authorities might not fully justify the forebodings expressed in the various surveys of 'the cuts'. We are only too aware, however, that our discussion of the consequences of the present Government's expenditure decisions for the PSS draws only on data for the first (part) year of its term of office. How the 1980/81 outturns will compare with previous years is not yet certain. The Secretary of State told the Select Committee that there were indications of 1980/81 spending levels being of the same order of magnitude in real terms as in 1979/80[69] — even though 1980/81 was, it will be recalled, the year in which the PSS were apparently intended to experience disproportionately large and absolute reductions in spending. What such a standstill in overall spending would mean for patterns of service outputs remains to be seen.

However, it seems scarcely possible that, nationally, the alarms of 1979 and 1980 will prove to have been fully justified (though their very expression may have contributed to their falsification) since spending at roughly 1979/80 levels would produce out-turns for 1980/81 some 8% above the Expenditure White Paper totals. On the other hand, a collective standstill on spending would mean rather more authorities experiencing cuts in base expenditure during 1980/81 than in 1979/80. It would also mean that PSS expenditure as a whole was below that calculated nationally as necessary to meet changes in levels and intensity of need (the 2% demographic growth allowance), or to finance the cost of commitments arising out of previous years' expenditure decisions. Moreover, it would be unwise to be complacent about levels of provision in relation to need, even in 1979/80. We have shown elsewhere that since 1974/75 the provision of both residential and community services failed to keep pace with the number of persons aged 65 and over and fell even further short of the increase in the number of over 75s.[70] The 'minor' client groups have a long history of neglect to make up and, despite increases in PSS provision, considerable numbers of the mentally ill and mentally handicapped remain in hospital because of the lack of alternative provision 'in the community'. If the situation of the PSS is less extreme than the Government's critics feared, there are still very real grounds for concern about the ability of these services to meet the demands placed upon them — particularly since the expected out-turns for 1980/81 imply an intensification (in relation to growth in need levels) of resource pressures on social services departments.

One factor in the 8% divergence between expenditure plans and out-turns has been the ambiguity of the Secretary of State's position. He has placed considerable emphasis on the indicative nature of the White Paper's guidelines for individual services within the tightly drawn limits for total local authority spending. However, it must be noted that this approach aroused, rather than cooled, passions among some LA personnel. What was seen as a 'nod and a wink' to ignore the Government's working assumption that PSS would be cut was experienced as an act of hyprocrisy rather than as a reprieve. Others subsequently claimed to be completely confused about the Minister's intentions since he had successively encouraged them 'to fight their corners' to minimize reductions in their own authorities (November 1979);[71] criticized them for overspending (June 1980);[72] and apparently congratulated them for having 'fought their corner extremely well' (September 1980).[73] These reactions underline the tensions inherent in an approach to local authority expenditure control based on 'non-enforced hypothecation'. From the local point of view it provides government with the luxury of taking stern measures while denying responsibility for the consequences. A more cynical but not necessarily less realistic assessment of the Secretary of State's approach is to place the PSS in the context of his total responsibilities. Reductions in expenditure, agreed with the Treasury, on Social Security and the NHS would have to be enforced since the Department is directly responsible for spending in these areas. The most successful defence of the DHSS budget as a whole, it may be argued, was, therefore, to load such cuts onto the PSS since the Minister could not be held responsible for overspendings in this case and the recent past history of the PSS suggested that a good many, if not all, departments might successfully engage in special pleading on behalf of the 'vulnerable' clients for whom they were pre-eminently responsible within the local authority sector. If this strategic approach to cuts was adopted in the DHSS it must be counted a success in the short-term. Its long-term success, however, depends upon the severity and effectiveness of expenditure constraint in local government.

For SSDs the problem is that, while the 'hypothecated' expenditures assumed in the calculation of RSG may not be enforced by government, they may still be implemented locally. Treasurers, resource committees and rival spending departments may be more responsive to the assumptions reflected in the RSG settlement than they are to subsequent statements by the ministers of spending departments.[74] Even if the White Paper cuts in PSS were primarily an exercise in budgetary expediency, therefore, the effects locally would not necessarily be cushioned by *ex post facto* reminders that LAs were free to make alternative distributions of resources, particularly as pressure intensifies.

Cuts: a preliminary conclusion. A definitive understanding of the nature and extent of cuts effected in any period is difficult to achieve and can only be attempted after the lapse of some time. Statistics take time to publish and at best tell a partial story. Nevertheless, the controversy over cuts can be placed into perspective, at least in a preliminary way, by reference to our typology of cuts.

Expenditure plans devised by the Government in 1979 and 1980 did not imply sustained cuts in the PSS budget in real terms, nor even the cessation of all growth. To this extent the reaction to these expenditure plans may indeed seem exaggerated, as ministers claimed. However, the expenditure policies did imply a cut in the planned rate of growth — to be achieved by a sharp cutback followed by the resumption of modest growth. This intended disruption of planned growth also threatened a cut in service cover. Even DHSS calculations assumed that a constant rate of growth of 2% would be necessary to offset the effects of demographic changes. The disruption of this pattern of growth, even for one year, would therefore lower the growth curve over a much longer period. Moreover, even a constant rate of growth could involve cuts in service cover nationally if, as seems likely, the 2% rate of growth failed fully to reflect increases in need. Local circumstances would determine the extent of local cuts, if any, in service cover.

Cuts in existing services could also be necessary even in a period of steady growth in real budgets if the revenue consequences of past changes — including the development of joint finance projects — were not fully reflected in growth. Similar consequences would follow from the effect of a 'volume squeeze' caused by rising unit costs and the failure of growth allocations fully to compensate for the effects of inflation.

Cuts in existing services would have seemed inevitable if the Government's expenditure policy had been implemented and growth had been interrupted. It is obviously possible that cuts made in existing services in order to accommodate the revenue consequences of new projects could skew resources systematically away from particular services or client groups — especially from those activities which prove easiest to cut in the short term. Finally, it must be added that the Government specifically advocated cuts in gross budgets in some service areas by recommending increases in charges as a way of coping with resource constraints. The implications of such changes could only be ascertained through close empirical observation.

Did any of these cuts emerge in practice, however? What we have shown is that the national pattern of protection afforded to the PSS by local authorities undermined these expenditure intentions: expenditure levels continued to grow in practice. Does this mean that the outcry against cuts was poorly founded? The paradoxical co-existence nationally of two realities — 'real growth' and 'real cuts' — is explained primarily by the problems of accommodating previously planned growth in reduced budgets — budgets which had to be pruned quickly and part way through the financial year 1979/80. Even a reduced level of growth, therefore, imposed a painful process of substitution of new developments for some existing forms of service. Such a process is not necessarily detrimental if the outcome is genuinely to be preferred, but there is a limit to how many older homes, for example, can be quickly closed to make room for more desirable new projects. There is also a limit to how far administration and 'bureaucracy' can be squeezed. Once these limits are exceeded, many of the easier cuts in existing services threaten key forms of community care — home help, meals on wheels, aids and adaptations.

Locally, the recent past experience of cuts has varied widely. Nationally, the problem has been essentially one of cuts in planned growth, probably in service cover, and the difficulty of making the kinds of substitutions noted above. The overwhelming conclusion, therefore, is that the real crisis could yet be to come. A continuation of the general pressure on local government expenditure must soon undermine the ability of local authorities to protect the PSS. Assuming that the easy adjustments have been made, cuts in existing service and in service cover would become inevitable in a service in which all clients fall within the 'most vulnerable' category.

SERVICE POLICIES

Change or continuity in policy?

The Government's approach to service policies during 1979 and 1980 was characterized by a virtual absence of policy initiatives. Expenditure policy largely precluded developments with resource implications, while governance policy placed limitations on the types of intervention which might be pursued even if resources were to be made available. But what of the service policy inheritance? Did the change of government produce changes in these policies or was it accompanied by continuity? Changes can be expressed either by asserting a new approach or by not implementing an inherited approach.

The Children and Young Persons Act, 1969, is the prime example of a policy which was effectively called into question by partial implementation during the Heath Administration and which is being more directly modified now through the tenor of the 'law and order debate' and by the proposed restoration of some powers to magistrates over the disposal of young offenders. Government policy in this area was set out in the White Paper *Young Offenders*.[75] Governmental guidance on expenditure constraints reminded local authorities of the high priority attached to law and order; the implication was that local priorities should change. This guidance, together with the exhortations to protect the most vulnerable, was indeed used locally to defend social service budgets. However, local authority acceptance of expenditure constraints had been conditional; it

53

was made clear that a moratorium would have to be imposed on new service responsibilities. A partial reconciliation of service and resource policies was therefore proposed in the form of an additional £2m (through RSG) to finance the court orders for residential care, and the additional demand for intermediate treatment, which was expected. Whether this will be sufficient to enable local authorities to implement the White Paper approach remains to be seen.

If only £2m was found to support a high priority policy in the law and order field, it is hardly surprising that the major feature of the personal social services was the absence of authoritative service policies. Until late 1980, policy initiatives was largely confined to 'zero cost' measures such as the consolidation of legislation in the fields of child care and fostering. The review of mental handicap policy, initiated by the previous Government, was completed in January 1980. It was apparently first seen by ministers in June 1980,[76] but was not published until December of that year. The Government had previously indicated, however, that resource scarcity precluded the implementation of the model of community care for the mentally handicapped advocated in the Report of the Jay Committee.[77] In a related field, the revision of Mental Health law — which the previous Government had put out to consultation — there was no evident progress. A similar delay also occurred in respect of policy for the elderly, despite the Secretary of State's commitment to publish a White Paper during 1980 in response to comments received on the Labour Government's consultative document *A Happier Old Age*.[78] Nevertheless, the overall impression was of a service policy vacuum. Few new policies emerged and policy continuity was brought into question by expenditure uncertainties.

Community care: a policy abandoned

The general, and fundamental, question raised by the existence of a policy vacuum is whether community care, the one service policy which has permeated all the major client groups in the personal social services, has itself been abandoned — by degrees and by default. Even if the broad principles underpinning past planning guidelines have not been repudiated, do they now make sense in the light of rapid, confusing and locally divergent changes in resource availability? Have expenditure constraints and the lack of co-ordination of resource and service policies fatally undermined community care? There have already been some calls for the explicit modification of the community care policy, at least in its guise as a social care alternative to NHS provision. The National Development Group for the Mentally Handicapped, for example, suggested that 'in the short term, health authorities may have to assume a greater responsibility for developing facilities in the community which local authorities could take over at a later date.'[79]

However, the malaise which now afflicts community care as a service policy is not merely the product of recent 'resource shock'. It also arises from the past tendency for resource policies to crowd out service policies and from the related tendency for 'policy implementation' to conceal the defects of service policies. The preoccupation with the instruments of planning had long obscured the crucial questions: why is community care believed to be more beneficial to clients; precisely what objectives should guide action and what results should be expected; what resource flows and levels of service are critical to the success of community care as a service policy?

Despite the fact that the Secretary of State conceded that it could potentially be threatened by resource constraints, community care continued to provide the apparent logic for decision making in the personal social services throughout the period under review. Had the confluence of Government policies therefore resulted in the 'implementation' of a policy which had essentially become devoid of meaning? As we have indicated, this was a question which needed to be asked throughout the late seventies; it was not the product merely of the actions of the new Conservative Government. But this only made an answer the more pressing. Without it, the personal social services were likely to be characterized by implementation as a substitute for policy and by resource policies which were innocent of service objectives. How, if at all, therefore, could community care be resuscitated within prevailing expenditure targets?

What was needed was a means of selectively injecting resources into developments congruent with the community care philosophy. In the absence of specific or hypothecated grants, the obvious mechanism was to expand Joint Finance. Although Joint Finance continued to be looked on favourably in 1979 and 1980, the limitations on its use had also begun to be apparent.[80] The capacity of local authorities to absorb the long-term costs arising from the productive use of Joint Finance was severely limited by the general climate of expenditure control. The only other way forward, canvassed by the NDG and by some directors of social services, would be to create a mechanism which permitted a larger, more permanent and direct transfer of resources from the NHS to the PSS. However, ministers had barely begun to respond to such thinking during 1980.[81]

CONSEQUENCES OF POLICIES IN RELATED FIELDS

The PSSC has noted that much of the workload of the PSS flows from decisions taken elsewhere, for example in the NHS, social security, housing, education and employment services.[82] We have already indicated that increased pressure falls upon the PSS at times of economic recession. A number of policy decisions in other fields may, therefore, also be expected to impact upon the administration of the PSS.

Legislation emanating from the DHSS itself — the NHS and Social Security Acts — was widely seen to have significance for the PSS.[83] In the case of the restructuring of the NHS, there was concern that, where coterminosity between health and local authorities was lost, NHS restructuring would significantly increase structural impediments to collaboration between them. It would also — in the pursuit of administrative savings within the NHS — impose greater administrative burdens upon local authorities and especially their SSDs. More fundamentally, it was feared that the new District Health Authorities would be dominated by the interests and management problems of the acute hospital sector at the expense of the long stay sectors where the need for collaboration to implement community care policies is particularly crucial. According to the Secretary of State, the 'main purpose' of restructuring was to encourage 'local initiatives, local decisions and local responsibility'.[84] It would be ironic if this policy of governance were to impede the implementation of any initiatives in the field of community care which ministers might subsequently wish to pursue. The need for compatibility between, and the reconciliation of, governance and service policies is no less important than that between resource and service policies.

In the field of social security a number of changes had wider implications. Local authorities were concerned, for example, that the reduction of discretionary payments in the supplementary benefit system would lead to increased demand for financial support under Section 1 of the 1963 Children and Young Persons Act which SSD budgets would be unable to meet. Another consequence of the same Act was the closing of a loophole whereby the costs of increased home help charges were simply transferred to the social security budget by supplementary benefit claimants. The ending of this procedure proved to be particularly troublesome for authorities which had planned to increase their charges in the expectation that local social security offices would meet such increases on behalf of claimants.

A final policy field in which Government decisions had important consequences for the PSS was that of housing. Various kinds of housing schemes funded both by the public and voluntary sectors have increasingly been advanced as essential components of community care programmes. Housing provision has been preferred both on cost-effectiveness grounds and as a more appropriate form of care than that provided in institutions. However, the very large reductions in the housing programme meant that only a very limited contribution to community care could be possible. Once again the status of community care as an explicit objective of service policy was brought into question by expenditure decisions.

V The Mixed Economy of Welfare: A Case Study

The PSS have always been characterized by a 'mixed economy' of statutory, voluntary, private and informal provision, and the balance to be struck between them is an important feature of personal social services policy. Current problems and policies have, in fact, highlighted this issue to such an extent that it is worth considering as a case study of policy interaction and implementation.

From the public expenditure perspective, the non-statutory sector may be seen both as an alternative source of resources (charitable giving and the 'free' labour of relatives, volunteers and altruistic neighbours) and as a more cost-effective user of some statutory resources. The Secretary of State has neatly summarized these assumptions: 'I tell [statutory services] that they can make their resources go very much further by working together with the voluntary bodies and all sorts of community groups'.[85] But this strand of interest in the non-statutory sector is not the preserve of this Government. The previous Labour Administration was by no means unsympathetic to the expansion of voluntarism, and the last Labour Secretary of State has restated his 'complete support for this concept'.[86] Unanimity in commitment can, of course, conceal party differences in philosophy. For example, Patrick Jenkin criticized the Labour Secretary of State's Good Neighbour Campaign for being overly dominated by the search for inexpensive forms of care and has repeatedly stressed that volunteers are not just a 'cheap pair of hands'. But both Secretaries of State have in practice been constrained to think in cost-effectiveness terms and to make resource arguments a central feature of their approach to the voluntary sector. This pragmatic approach to the non-statutory sector has greatly clouded the underlying issues.

In order to proceed, we need to examine some of the fundamental questions which could or should underpin policy developments. We shall be best able to do this if we first outline the development of ideas about non-statutory welfare during the last decade or so.

Voluntary social action: in search of a policy

During the past decade a process of change has occurred which can now be labelled as the 'collapse of the pure doctrine of state welfare'.[87] This does not mean that state social provision is in decline in absolute terms. What it does mean is that state provision is no longer always seen as a sufficient, necessary, or unambiguously desirable way of responding to social problems. The parallel event is a regeneration of interest in the extent, nature, limits and role of non-statutory forms of social service provision and social care. This level of interest has been reflected in the work and conclusions of four major committees of enquiry, as well as in an increased flow of academic research and writing. In chronological order of publication, the reports which arose from those committees were: Seebohm, 1968; Aves, 1969; Goodman, 1976; and Wolfenden, 1978. The first was an official, government-sponsored committee of enquiry concerned primarily with statutory services and only tangentially with non-statutory social provision, while the others were all non-governmental committees funded by private foundations to study particular aspects of the role of voluntary action in social policy. Each of them concentrated upon the personal social services.

The term voluntary social action is used here to refer to the entire field of activity of voluntary organizations and organized volunteer work; there is no intention of implying that voluntary social action is a cohesive social movement. It is particularly important to differentiate between voluntary organizations and volunteers, or voluntarism. Some voluntary organizations — especially the largest, oldest and most specialized — rely substantially, or exclusively, on paid (often fully professional) personnel to deliver social work, residential, day-care and domiciliary services. Others depend heavily, or primarily, on volunteer workers. Although volunteers are primarily deployed by voluntary organizations, their use in statutory services has been growing — to varying degrees — for some years.

The ideological background. Before turning to the reports, let us briefly note the issues of ideology and philosophy alluded to earlier. Although much state social provision is traditionally seen to have originated directly from voluntary social action, the relationship has been ideologically contentious. Advocates of state social services have emphasised the role of voluntary social action as a vehicle 'for upper and middle class philanthropy appropriate to the social structure of Victorian Britain'[88] and as underpinning a social policy of 'state deterrence'.[89] The impact — not least symbolically — of repressive, socially divisive or paternalistic philosophies, and the work of the Charity Organization Society in particular,[90] served to tar the whole of voluntary social action with the same brush. This tendency to treat the entire range of non-statutory social action as part of an apparently homogeneous 'voluntary sector' continues to bedevil analysis and policy making.

The reaction against the stereotype of voluntary provision certainly helped to cement the surprisingly cohesive and widely accepted 'pure doctrine' of state welfare which underpinned the development of the post-war 'welfare state'. The most effective and acceptable response to social problems was seen to involve comprehensive state social services, which were necessarily large bureaucracies, and which operated through paid employees — ideally with professional training and status. This reliance on state, bureaucratic, professional, service production was seen to be both necessary and sufficient. At best, voluntary social action was seen to be, ideally, unnecessary; at worst, as retrogressive and a threat to the adequacy of state provision.

Although this picture is over-simplified, the significance of the shift in ideologies is that each of these assumptions has been challenged — for a variety of reasons. It would be surprising if such disparate forces were automatically to produce an ideal balance between state and non-statutory services, a coherent new philosophy on which to base future social policy, or a resolution of conflicts (of interest and perception) and practical problems. It is in this context that one must examine the reports noted above. Did they provide a firm foundation for change and development?

Seebohm: the statutory perspective. Because the brief was to redesign state social welfare services, the Seebohm Committee only considered non-statutory social care in passing. The Report noted the demise of the 'Victorian philosophy', while warning that 'remnants of [the] old practices and attitudes remain in the condescension and social exclusiveness of a few voluntary organizations and in the suspicion and mistrust of some local authorities'.[91] In short, past sins had been expiated in general and should no longer be used as a barrier to the systematic development of 'the voluntary sector', but particular voluntary organizations remained problematic, as did the absence of a new, positive philosophy on which trust and mutual respect could be based. The Seebohm Report also noted what is now universally acknowledged but not readily quantified: the emergence of many new voluntary organizations devoted to collective self-help (organizations of clients, patients or people in need, or their relatives), to the provision of information and advocacy services, and to the criticism of social policy by revealing unmet needs, deficiencies and inappropriate responses — the vast majority of this criticism being levelled at statutory policies and services. But these issues were not pursued. In the space of six paragraphs, the Seebohm Report simply outlined the dimensions of voluntary social action which would need to be examined more fully elsewhere.

Aves: volunteers and voluntarism. The Aves Committee considered three main issues: the role of volunteer workers (which had received little attention at that time); the relationship of volunteers to professional workers and to the formal social services; and the appropriateness of contemporary practice in the fields of volunteer recruitment, training and deployment.

The Committee was faced by the legacy of the post-war disinterest in voluntarism: it was not even possible to describe the extent, range, variety and context of volunteer work. Any analysis of the function and the utility of voluntarism would have to be built upon such basic description. Although the Committee undertook only a small amount of investigation, it effectively highlighted the depth of our ignorance and proceeded to collate existing and newly emerging material.

The stereotype of voluntarism as a form of middle-class imperialism, carried forward by middle-aged women, was rejected and partially demolished.[92] While the available evidence tended to confirm the predominance of the middle classes among formal volunteers, informal and neighbourly care networks were noted as possibly the more usual pattern of working class behaviour. The growth of mutual aid groups and organizations was thought to cut across class boundaries.[93] The estimated 10% of the population involved in some form of voluntary action was seen to include far more men and a much wider age range than the stereotype would suggest.[94] In short, the heterogeneity of volunteer activity was advanced in defence of its legitimacy.

Although not deeply analytical, the examination of volunteer motivation suggested that volunteers themselves strongly rejected the image of 'do-gooding paternalism' and recognized a complex interplay of altruistic and self-oriented considerations — and of satisfactions and frustrations in the 'helping role'.

The Committee therefore laid the tentative basis for a rehabilitation of volunteer work within the British philosophy of social welfare and indicated the need for an analytical sociology of voluntarism. It also raised some of the policy questions which needed to be answered. The relationship between volunteer and professional workers was shown to be highly variable and frequently problematic. Similarly, the distribution of volunteer work was shown to be uneven as between different need groups and geographical areas. With notable exceptions, the boundary between social work and voluntarism was seen to reflect the differential attractiveness of client groups to social workers, rather than a division of tasks. The volunteer role was apparently shaped by the process of professionalization and not the particular contributions which professionals and volunteers might make. One form of task differentiation which was noted — the allocation of 'menial' work to volunteers — caused concern. The maintenance of formal social services through the use of cheap labour was not the Aves Committee's view of the role of volunteers and voluntarism.[95]

A number of the policy and administrative issues raised by the Aves Report have been at the centre of subsequent development: local and central government have become more involved — not least financially — in volunteer work; the number of full-time organizers of volunteer work has increased considerably; and training and administrative practices have received more attention. The latter area of development has been fostered in particular by the work of the Volunteer Centre, an independent national 'resource centre' which the Aves Report called for almost as an after-thought.

Nevertheless, and despite the growth in the importance of volunteers 'on the ground' and in public policy, the basic analysis of voluntarism had only begun to gain the momentum which might have been expected. By the time the present Government came into office, research had lagged well behind the upsurge in discussion and in expectations. Most of the critical issues were at the stage of initial exploration: the extent, distribution, intensity and effectiveness of organized volunteer — and informal — care; the exploration of individual motivation and of social contexts conducive to voluntarism; the pattern of benefits and dis-benefits generated; and the multiple legitimations — and ideologies — of voluntarism deployed in the debate and policy making.[96] Voluntarism seemed to be alive and well, perhaps over-hastily rehabilitated in public policy, but little understood.

Goodman: charities and charitable status. The Goodman Committee ploughed its way through the law and legal precedent surrounding the contentious issue of which kinds of organizations should be accorded charitable status. Few changes were suggested.

Charitable status brings three main forms of tax advantage: exemptions from direct taxation; exemptions from indirect taxation; and tax reliefs granted on contributions made by individuals and companies. What the Goodman Report[97] failed to acknowledge fully is that charitable status is a matter of public concern precisely because public monies are involved. To examine the purposes supported by charities is to act as a 'social policy archeologist'; one's 'dig' reveals the sedimented values and norms of centuries.

In an admittedly trenchant and polemical way, the minority report by Ben Whitaker raised the policy issues which the main report avoided. Why, he asked, should the taxpayer be compelled to contribute to charities which exist to restrict the freedom of citizens to be entertained on Sundays, or to the preservation of silverware in officers' messes? In an attempt to concentrate private giving and state subsidies, Whitaker proposed a new and stringent criterion for charitable status: that it should be confined to those organizations which concentrate primarily on 'deprivation and the disadvantaged'. Quite apart from the incipient philistinism involved in a comprehensive withdrawal of privileges from the arts and similar cultural purposes, it is questionable whether Whitaker's approach would, in fact, increase the flow of resources to social welfare. Even if successful, such a policy would have the disadvantage of exacerbating the unequal

61

distribution of voluntary provision: the elderly, the physically disabled and children are 'marketable' need groups — many are not. The merit of Whitaker's position, therefore, is not the conclusions it yielded but the policy issues which it exposed. The Goodman Report (majority) failed to identify such issues or to annunciate policy principles, as opposed to refurbished legal arrangements.

Wolfenden: voluntary organizations. The Wolfenden Committee had the widest brief of the three and it fully recognized the historical legacy of hostility and mistrust, as well as of partnership and co-operative working.[98] Did it provide an adequate and comprehensive basis for future development and problem solving?

The Committee's first and enduring contribution was to initiate a substantial body of research. Virtually no systematic information has been available on any of the major issues: size and composition; role and functions; manpower resources (paid and volunteer); financial position; or policy intentions of voluntary organizations. Much of the research initiated by the Committee was published separately, but the Report supplied some welcome factual material. It confirmed that, in the personal social services, volunteer workers providing service to clients through voluntary organizations probably amount to a larger work force than the paid staff in the local authority social services department: approximately 260,000 full-time equivalent volunteers compared with 200,000 paid staff.[99] It was also known that, in addition, voluntary organizations employ a minimum of 20,000 paid staff[100] (the majority working directly with clients), and the statutory services also use volunteers. The combined manpower effect of voluntary social action must, therefore, substantially exceed that of paid personnel in the statutory services. By no means all this activity is of a traditional service-giving kind involving a sharp distinction between 'helpers' and 'helped', however. The Wolfenden Committee confirmed the rapid diversification of voluntary effort into other roles: information, advice, advocacy, political action and mutual or collective self-help. Unfortunately, no hard data were reported on the relative importance of these roles within different organizations, within different need areas, or within the corpus of voluntary organizations taken as a whole.

At the ideological or philosophical level, therefore, it could be asserted that 'the voluntary sector' was no longer to be seen as detrimental to the maintenance of a healthy state commitment — perhaps the reverse; but detail was absent. This deficiency was reflected in the major plank of the Wolfenden proto-philosophy of post welfare state social policy. The Committee implied that voluntary organizations were entirely beneficial, on the twin assumptions that state-voluntary relationships were characterized by partnerships and that voluntary action reinforced the pluralistic nature of society. Here we begin — all too soon — to discern the defects of analysis on the report. Once it moved beyond the presentation of new and useful data, the document became embroiled in the fuzzy platitudes which bedevil this field. For example, what does partnership mean and how could one detect a failure to develop it? Does partnership imply that voluntary organizations ought only to do those things which build upon the basic state system?

The recent experience in the United States has cast a pall over the interesting notion of 'purposive duplication', but surely this was a concept with which to explore statutory-voluntary relationships in Britain? Administrative studies have been obsessed with co-ordination and administrative neatness; social service reform has followed suit, and the Wolfenden Committee seemed to have been similarly preoccupied. But given the fact of untidiness — which may or may not equal pluralism — would it not have been worthwhile to test for genuine competitiveness and its consequences? At least the intellectual contribution of asking how this could be done would have been worthwhile. A rigorously analytical approach was needed to the development of a policy for voluntary provision. Wolfenden did not fully provide it. Roles and relationships were analysed but no clear commitments, criteria of evaluation, or strategies, emerged.

The major proposal by Wolfenden which attracted attention was that of central government funding for 'intermediary bodies' (voluntary organizations, local or national, which, rather than supplying a service directly to the public, exercise one or more of the following functions in relation to the voluntary sector: development; support services; liaison and representation). Their claim was, *inter alia,* that strengthening these functions would help reduce the unevenness of voluntary provision, and this could well be true. Equally important, more financial support for the voluntary sector was applauded, given the trend towards a reduced real value of charitable giving by the public. Whether 'co-ordinative' functions should be the priority target of extra government support is debatable, as is the wisdom of increasing the level of dependence on state finance. However, the Wolfenden Committee could identify no alternative sources of funding and they had to rely on the Goodman Committee's study of charitable status for a major part of their (rather pessimistic) conclusions on finance.

Financial and administrative issues are undoubtedly of great importance, but if the broader questions and issues were lost in a much narrower debate about money, the wider opportunity would have been neglected. The Labour Government's response to Wolfenden's call for a long-term strategy suggested that this was precisely what would happen.[101] The major hope was that the research and enquiry which had been stimulated would push the fundamental issues to the fore.

Welfare pluralism: solution or slogan?

The publication of the Wolfenden Report did in fact give a considerable impetus to study and debate. In particular, Wolfenden's concept of welfare pluralism has been taken up and used as a guiding principle for, no less, the reshaping of welfare provision as a whole. However, as is often the case in public policy, the issues have not been pursued through the tidy and sequential analytical process implied in notions of rational policy-making. 'Welfare pluralism' has rapidly gained ground as a generalized 'solution', broadly interpreted to mean increased support for and development of non-statutory services. Unfortunately, the analysis of underlying problems has lagged behind. We appear to have a 'solution' to a miscellany of often imprecisely defined problems.

The confusion is compounded, however, by the amorphous nature of the solution itself: what does welfare pluralism mean? If the existing 'mixed economy' is inadequate, what is it that will make the crucial difference? Is there a 'critical mass' of non-statutory provision which will move our present system towards an appropriate state of 'welfare pluralism', or do we need to look for a powerful development of particular kinds of non-statutory growth? If the latter, which kinds are deemed to be crucial? The imprecision of the present prescription is revealed by the lack of specificity about the optimal mix to be sought within the non-statutory sector. What rate and direction of change is desirable in formal voluntary organizations, mutual aid groups, volunteer activity, informal and neighbourly care, and private (profit motivated) provision? One of the more fully developed advocacies of welfare pluralism, that produced by the National Council for Voluntary Organizations, certainly assumes that a substantial expansion of private provision is neither a feasible nor a desirable option, but the relative contribution expected from the remaining elements of the non-statutory 'sector' remains vague.[102] The impression gained from the current state of discussion is that almost any form and pattern of growth is to be welcomed providing it occurs outside the state social services system.

The lack of concise analysis and rationally-formulated public policy may prove to be a prime example of a possibility which we raised at the beginning of this monograph: that policy may in practice be far less crucial in affecting change than the modification of assumptive worlds. Uncertainty and confusion may be the prime stimulus for breaking the mould of established behaviour. However, if we are to understand what is happening and to sketch the outline of an intellectual map on which to plot the impact of the present Government's tenure of office, we need to approximate the classical rational-analysis mode of thinking. Let us therefore begin by examining the problems which are currently being diagnosed as justification for the idea of welfare pluralism.

Problems to be overcome. The first and most popular basis for advocating some form of 'welfare pluralism' is to emphasise and castigate the 'failure of the welfare state'. The difficulty with this approach is that it readily degenerates into a ragbag of over-generalized statements of empirically diagnosed deficiencies (e.g., the professionalization of care can exacerbate, rather than resolve, social ills), repudiations of past objectives and methods of social provision (e.g., the rejection of equality as a goal and centralized planning as a means), and the assertion of dubious relationships between state social services and wider public issues (e.g., the notion that 'the welfare state' undermines the responsibility of the individual and therefore the moral and economic state of the nation). The welfare state has not infrequently been simultaneously criticized for failing to achieve its presumed objectives — not least because of a lack of resources — and for possessing those presumed objectives in the first place; the personal social services and social work are not exempt. Precisely because the 'failure of the welfare state' approach is riven with inconsistencies and lack of intellectual rigour, it is a powerful tool in changing climates of opinion as opposed to devising specific policies.

Nevertheless, when it comes to policy formation, some statements of underlying problems are likely to be given greater credence than others, explicitly or implicitly. Let us therefore specify several of the diagnoses which could underpin an interest in welfare pluralism and note their implications. One could argue that the main problem facing the personal social services is the level of present and future unmet need. The solution would be to expand the sum total of care by whatever means this care could be most appropriately attained. The classical response would have been only to demand more public expenditure. The realistic response for the medium term is certainly to look for ways of using existing public expenditure more effectively, while also attracting new resources. However, the general gist of emphasising need is clear — it means that our problem is that of obtaining more resources: expanding the non-statutory sector may or may not make a large contribution to this objective in different fields of action and with different client groups.

The second and closely related perspective is to emphasise the importance of cost effectiveness, and Bleddyn Davies has strongly argued that one of the implications of the 'cost effectiveness imperative' is to make much greater use of volunteers and 'good neighbours'.[103] But the central question which then faces us is: in what circumstances can non-statutory provision offer services of the same quality and acceptability as the state at a lower cost or, alternatively, in what circumstances can services of a reduced but agreed level of quality be offered at a lower cost? This approach clearly implies a systematic pattern of substitutability between different forms of care, with cost-effectiveness as the main criterion for choice.

65

The third possibility is that our problem is not merely need, nor scarcity, but the changing nature of need. Roy Parker has given particular emphasis to the growing demands placed upon our society by the volume of need for what he calls 'tending'.[104] The tending role is increasingly becoming an issue of social policy because of the growth in the need for it, and because of changes in sex role stereotyping and sex role behaviour.

The fourth issue, underlined by Roy Parker's analysis and now being pursued in detail, is that of the caring capacity of the community.[105] The questions which arise concern the extent to which the caring capacity of the community is changing; the directions of any changes; and the possibility of stimulating the caring capacity in terms of volume and quality. The implications for non-statutory welfare of the changing nature of need and the caring capacity of the community are only just beginning to be explored in any depth.

A fifth way of specifying the problems before us is to emphasise the cost to carers (kin, friends and 'volunteers') of providing informal voluntary care. Are these costs acceptable? Are they changing and can they be mitigated? The implication of focusing on this issue, as in the previous example, is that both the statutory sector and the formal voluntary organizations may need to change the ways in which they work and the relationships which they have traditionally adopted to the informal care sector so as to provide a pattern of supportive services.

The sixth problem area is captured in the criticisms of services as rigid, impersonal, 'bureaucratic' and unresponsive to clients. There are several underlying dimensions to this criticism which need to be separately identified: the scale and uniformity of services; the extent to which, and ways in which, an equitable distribution of service is pursued; the means of exercising public accountability, not least for public expenditure; the use made of stultifying, or liberating, forms of organization; and the extent and nature of centralization and decentralization in service planning and management. In the absence of good evidence, none of these issues should be regarded as inherently a problem in state services and inherently avoidable in non-statutory services. The implications of this grouping of problems for the mixed economy of welfare is essentially open to debate and empirical study.

The last problem area noted above is central to the NCVO argument, but it can lead to an even more fundamental specification of the problem as that of economic monopoly. The state can be seen as a quasi-monopolistic supplier of social services. There are alternatives, but they are weak and underdeveloped. The advocacy of welfare pluralism could, therefore, be taken to imply the need for purposive duplication: the non-statutory sector should be stimulated to provide choice and competition. The choice could be either between the state and the non-statutory sector or within the non-statutory sector itself. The pursuit of purposive duplication is an important possibility and it ought not to be ignored or belittled. There is clearly a sense in which some non-statutory social services are already 'competing' with state provision and the question is not whether some element of purposive duplication is legitimate but how far it should be extended (and how far it is undermined by expenditure cuts). It could, in principle, be extended to all social services and all localities or it could be confined to demonstration projects which are designed to challenge the monopoly of the state in key sectors and thereby produce innovations which could subsequently be generalized throughout the state or the non-statutory services. The notion of using the non-statutory sector to produce competitive social services runs into most of the criticisms levelled at the arguments for returning to the market, with the important exception than non-statutory provision does not involve the cash nexus — the profit motive.

The final problem is that of political monopoly. One of the main ways in which welfare pluralism is defended is by asserting that a state monopoly of social service provision is harmful to the fabric of our political system. [106] Once one has acknowledged that there is a prima facie case to be answered, however, one must ask where one believes power is presently concentrated. Is it in the hands of the state *per se?* Is it in the hands of bureaucrats or professions who run state services? Is it in the hands of classes, elites or privileged categories of people who gain most from the existence of state services? Having answered these questions, we would then need to consider which of these problems could be resolved by expanding the non-statutory sector and which could potentially be resolved within the state sector itself. Clearly, if concentration of power in the hands of the state is the problem, an expansion of the non-statutory sector could conceivably be a solution and reform of state services would not be an alternative. However, it is not beyond dispute that the non-statutory sector could avoid a concentration of power in the hands of bureaucrats, nor that reform of the state would be impossible in this respect. Similarly, while a concentration of power in the hands of professionals may be offset by the development of informal and volunteer service, many formal voluntary organizations are as heavily dependent as in the state on professional service providers.

Welfare pluralism is not an unambiguous solution to the different facets of power concentration noted above. However, we should go further and ask whether the real task is that of increasing citizens' control over their 'life-space'. If this is the nub, the solution may lay well outside the sphere of the personal social services. We may then be talking primarily about the distribution of employment opportunities and of incomes within a society which is increasingly characterized by instability and uncertainty in employment. Depending upon how one perceives the problem of power, welfare pluralism could be a central or tangential response, or a dangerous red herring. The precise content and form of welfare pluralism is not irrelevant, either.

The critique of social planning. Political rhetoric conceals the back-room work of government departments until the day that specific policies are launched into the arena of public discussion. The present Government may therefore be well advanced in its delineation and weighting of problems of the kind outlined above, but a generally confused consideration of issues presently characterizes public debate. This can best be illustrated by noting the treatment accorded to one of the perceived 'failures' of state welfare: social planning.

The Government's stance on governance policy naturally predisposes it against centralized and bureaucratic planning. To attack 'dirigiste' social planning is to push responsibility 'back where it belongs': in the hands of local, decentralized decison-makers. It is also to cut bureaucracy and to thin the 'swollen' ranks of the civil service. It is perhaps more surprising to find the same general critique of past social planning coming from leading figures in the voluntary sector.[107] In this case, however, the criticism is importantly modified by a defence of equity and social justice as the value base of social policy. There are obviously choices to be made between styles of planning and management, and governance policy is a field in which genuine political divergence can occur. But is the advocacy of welfare pluralism as an antidote to 'dirigiste' state social planning well-founded on logical argument?

Is it the case that British social planning has been dirigiste? Gladstone uses both French and East European examples when discussing dirigism, but he gives few examples of dirigiste planning in Britain.[108] He does mention planning within the National Health Service and the considerable degree of centralization which it is assumed has occurred within this service. By way of contrast, the Government presented its proposals for restructuring the NHS as designed to serve a decentralization of power. But is this necessarily a benefit and, if so, to whom?[109] The loss of the area health authority within a restructured health service could well mean an increased concentration of power in hospitals, in the acute medical specialisms, and in the regional health authorities (not to mention the DHSS).[110] Not that these various institutions and groups should not have power, but shifts of power in their direction are also likely to involve shifts of power away from the 'Cinderella' client groups. If this is the practical outcome of restructuring the health service, the apparently benign and attractive notions of pluralism and decentralization could simply mean a relocation of power and a further erosion of the position of those client groups which have been given some increased priority in recent years by means of 'centralized' social planning. Neither centralization nor decentralization should be treated as absolute values. The 'decentralization' embodied in the structural reform of the health service, for example, is quite different from that arising through resource transfers from health to local authority services (e.g., through Joint Financing or other mechanisms currently under consideration).

Perhaps what is intended in the application of the epithet 'dirigiste' to social planning is simply the drawing of an instructive comparison. The achievement of non-statutory pluralism, it could be argued, would permit us to avoid bureaucratic dysfunction and the amassing of power. But would it? Would only a minimum of bureaucratic organization and planning in fact permit us to ensure equity and, conversely, is it possible to pursue equity without establishing at least a body of centralized power and control? In short, we must begin to distinguish between:

the auspices,
the objectives and values, and
the form of social service provision.

In particular, there is a need to consider whether certain forms of service organization are necessary to the pursuit of certain objectives, regardless of who actually provides the service. Put as a question, is it the case that what has been labelled as dirigism is in fact associated with state social services only because the state has become the guardian of equity and that the pursuit of equity on a national scale in mass-produced services has required a considerable degree of centralist control of resources and of forward planning? In other words, can the non-statutory system provide mass-produced services, preserve equity, and at the same time avoid 'dirigism'? Is there an inherent merit in the non-statutory sector which would ensure that these objectives could be simultaneously achieved in a way in which they cannot within the state services? Examples from other European countries in which welfare pluralism is well entrenched do not give great reason for optimism.[111]

What is welfare pluralism? We have tried to indicate that there are diverse arguments to suggest that state provision of personal social services should be subject to close scrutiny. Some of these are based on the perception that state provision is not a *sufficient* solution, both in the sense of being under-resourced and of being but one element in a necessarily diverse pattern of responses to social need. Other arguments tend to suggest that state provision is not a *necessary* solution and that non-statutory provision could be greatly expanded as a substitute for state services.

A rather different approach treats such considerations as epiphenomenal and concentrates on social values and ideologies. There is a strong tendency within the present Government to emphasise individualism and social obligation and thereby to minimize the importance of social rights and collective action. It is a theme which highlights the relevance of informal care by kin. But it poses questions about the value base of non-statutory care and the environment in which it best survives. How far are voluntary organizations and informal care a form of collective action which flourish within a framework of state commitment

69

to social need, and how far do they gain sustenance from being an alternative to, or repudiation of, collective action and state provision? Once again, there is a major conflation of issues: collective action and the values which underpin it tend to be identified exclusively with state services.

Running beneath these more philosophical perspectives is an apparently non-ideological and practical commitment to cut or contain public expenditure. It raises questions about the caring capacity of the alternatives to state provision, their independence in reality of public expenditure and their dependence or otherwise on an infra-structure of state services.

Have these various strands been woven into a coherent set of propositions about the nature and role of welfare pluralism? The state of Government thinking will be examined below, but let us first consider the proposals advocated from within the voluntary sector which begin to provide one framework for policy formation. Francis Gladstone has identified two ways forward: by way of selective, pilot extensions of non-statutory provision; and by way of 'blanket gradualist pluralism.'[112] His clear preference is for the latter, but what does it mean? At least three possible meanings could be attributed to this prescription.

The first is that there should be a general expansion of the non-statutory sector as a net addition to those services currently existing and provided for by the state. While entirely laudable in many ways, this objective implies a substantial and permanent increase in public expenditure — unless non-statutory expansion can be self-supporting in the long term.

The second possibility is a general but partial replacement of existing statutory services so as to produce a mixture of statutory and non-statutory in all or most fields of provision — a mixture less 'dominated' by the state than is the case at present. This is implied in much of the discussion of welfare pluralism. It would presumably mean at least a temporary increase in public expenditure; in the long term, public expenditure might in fact be reduced or maintained at a stable level.

The third possibility is a gradual but total replacement of the state, at least in selected areas of welfare provision. It is not at all clear that this is what advocates of welfare pluralism have in mind, but the logic of the NCVO case, and of Francis Gladstone's book, does point in this direction. Both these publications produce an apparently systematic expose of the 'failure' of the welfare state. Presumably, a welfare state which has been such a conspicuous source of failure merits fairly substantial, if not total, replacement; alternatively, it is possible that a significant shift to the non-statutory sector could be seen as a means of revitalizing the remaining state system (by challenging its status as a monopolistic supplier).

It may reasonably be assumed that the concept of blanket gradualist pluralism favoured by the NCVO is in fact a combination of the first and a modified version of the second: an expansion of the non-statutory sector as a net addition to existing services *and* as a selective and partial replacement for existing state services. However, there is also a tendency to take an altogether simpler line and to hope that with encouragement a 'thousand flowers will bloom' with unpredictable, but beneficial, results.

As it presently stands, however, the case for blanket gradualist pluralism runs a number of risks. For example, it

tends to sound like a case of special pleading for the voluntary sector in hard times, at the expense of the state sector;

lacks the specific content and proposals needed to take us beyond simply producing 'more of the same' in the non-statutory sector;

tends to take as given the virtues claimed for the non-statutory sector — which are poorly tested (e.g., the opportunities for 'participation' through, and the cost effectiveness of, non-statutory provision);

denies these same virtues to the statutory sector and potentially distracts attention from the need to transform, rather than transcend, the state as a provider of services;

assumes that the virtues claimed for the non-statutory sector will survive the strains of expansion and that non-statutory provision is and will remain relatively uncontaminated by the ills which are said to beset state services (e.g., impersonal and inflexible service, 'trade union mindedness', and spiralling costs).

The alternative approach of mounting selected pilot experiments embracing specific objectives and including a commitment to monitoring and evaluation is apparently much less adventurous. However, it would have the advantage, in principle, of requiring clarity on the major issues which we have identified in this section: the nature of the problems which are felt to be most in need of resolution: the values and objectives to be maximized; and the incompatibilities of values and objectives which are likely to arise and the choices which ought therefore to be faced. However, these desiderata are not exclusive to the experimental approach to change. There are choices to be made in both the content and style of public policy-making towards the personal social services.

Welfare pluralism and Government policy

The notion of welfare pluralism clearly accords well with a number of pre-occupations of the present Government — not least while both are stated in general terms. By comparison with the prescriptions of academics and the voluntary sector, however, Government policy has followed a curiously muted and largely unspecific course to date. Nevertheless, several themes are clear.

For example, the non-statutory sector is central to the notion of disengagement by the state: 'We must do more to help people to help themselves, and families to look after their own. We must also encourage the voluntary movement and self-help groups working in partnership with statutory service'.[113] What a Labour Government might have sought for reasons of resource scarcity, the present Government also perceives as desirable on quite other grounds. At this point, however, ambiguities in the governance and resource strands of thinking begin to pose sharp and inconvenient dilemmas for policy implementation. If a pluralist society characterized by substantial state disengagement is desired, the autonomy and financial independence of the non-statutory sector is paramount — as members of the Government have emphasised. On the other hand, if the non-statutory sector is to be seen as an expanding and effective source of care, two issues have to be faced: the considerable and continuing dependence of voluntary provision on state financial support; and the desirability of co-ordination both within and between the non-statutory and statutory sectors. The notion of 'partnership' can readily become a synonym for 'dirigiste planning' or, at the other extreme, for haphazard overlap and duplication.

The Wolfenden Committee made proposals which a Labour Government might have accepted and implemented without too many misgivings. The pluralist ideal was to be reconciled with the warm embrace of public money through the good offices of 'intermediary bodies' — voluntary organizations with a capacity for stimulating and co-ordinating development. Charitable giving was not perceived to be an adequate financial base for voluntary bodies and the need for public support was therefore seen to be a general one, but it was to be channelled in particular into the strengthening of intermediary bodies and functions. Both elements of the Wolfenden solution could be expected to raise dubieties in the minds of Conservative ministers: it implied a significant increase in public expenditure on the voluntary sector and a possible extension of the co-ordinative, system-integrative values of the planner. The danger, if not the intention, could be that state services would merely become the hub of a more fully articulated system subsuming the non-statutory sector.

Differences in philosophy centre on the location of the 'centre of gravity' in the 'mixed economy' and therefore on the role of the state. For example, the Labour Home Secretary, Merlyn Rees, while describing voluntary organizations as 'the essential partners of the statutory authorities' went on to describe them very much as additions to the statutory services: 'Whatever the scale of statutory provision, we cannot do without the *extra* contribution from the voluntary sector'.[114] Patrick Jenkin's approach, on the other hand, was to argue that: 'We cannot operate as if the statutory services are the central provider with a few volunteers here and there to back them up'.[115] What was also important about Jenkin's approach was that the voluntary organizations themselves were not to move to the centre of the stage: 'We should recognize that the informal sector lies at the centre with statutory services and the organized voluntary sector providing backup, expertise and support'.[116] Voluntary bureaucracies are thus seen to be no more acceptable than statutory ones. This emphasis upon the centrality of informal systems of care based on the family and neighbourhood is an important distinguishing feature between the two administrations and it is in accord with much thinking in the voluntary sector itself. This is not to say that the importance of informal care was not recognized previously, but that in comparison with statutory services it was accorded a less pre-eminent position.

Is there a coherent policy? A coherent service policy for the 'mixed economy' of the personal social services would need to include principles governing: the respective roles of each form of provision (statutory, voluntary, private and informal); the relative scale and scope of the contribution to be expected from each; and the nature of the relationship between them. Such a policy would provide a basis for systematic implementation.

The conventional wisdom of recent decades has been that non-statutory provision should complement state services. Interpreting this phrase is difficult, but certain assumptions have been clear enough. The state has been seen as the provider of basic services and 'gap filling' has not been seen as a legitimate role for the non-statutory sector. A more positive statement of the non-statutory role would typically include references to pioneering of new services which are qualitatively different from those available through the state. The notion of voluntary provision complementing that of the state does in fact suggest a service policy rationale, albeit somewhat imprecise. Has government policy specified more fully, or modified, this conventional statement of roles?

That change in the role of the state can be contemplated is clear. The Head of the Social Work Service has argued, for example:

> I do not therefore have difficulty in accepting the role of the State as residual . . . the voluntary sector must to some extent return to providing and paying for services which we have come to expect from the State. This cannot in practice mean a large shift in responsibility but it will represent a departure from the values of the past decade.[117]

Initially, Patrick Jenkin spoke of the role of the statutory sector as 'a backup to informal and formal voluntary effort . . . a long stop for the very special needs going beyond the range of voluntary services'.[118] In principle, this statement could imply a long-term reversal of statutory and non-statutory roles, with an expanded non-statutory sector meeting the major part of basic need.

As we have shown, the approach advocated by the National Council for

Voluntary Organizations would certainly involve such a long-term role reversal: much statutory provision of services is seen to have limited relevance to future development.[119] The merit of their proposals, however, is that specific functions are allocated to the state — most notably the redistribution of resources to disadvantaged groups and the pursuit of equity between client groups and between different geographical areas. The Government, by comparison, seemed still to be searching for a clear view of the role of the state. Indeed, Patrick Jenkin suggested that the appropriate strategy might be the pragmatic one of 'stimulating the voluntary, and informal and the private sector [and, thereby, to] clarify the role of the statutory sector'.[120] He also indicated that the need for statutory services would be subject to local variation as non-statutory care 'is unlikely ever to spread uniformly across the country'.[121]

Implementing a shift in the centre of gravity. Despite the lack of detail, certain policy objectives have been espoused: the expansion of voluntary and informal social care and increased support for this development from social services departments. How could such objectives be achieved? In considering the problem of expanding and strengthening voluntary social services, at least three preconditions can be identified: the creation of a supportive philosophical environment; the stimulation of innovation and service development within the voluntary sector; and the expansion of voluntary organizations' funds.

Ministerial speeches have clearly gone a long way towards fulfilling the first of these. The second depends primarily upon spontaneous action within the voluntary sector, but the Wolfenden emphasis on the development function of intermediary bodies has been taken up on a small and experimental basis by the Voluntary Services Unit in the Home Office. The third is perhaps the most fundamental, and it illustrates most clearly the problems of implementation.

Voluntary organizations gain funds from two principal sources — charitable giving and the public sector. The present Government hoped for a significant expansion in charitable giving, and a number of changes in fiscal policy have been urged upon it to bring this about. However, the initial effect of fiscal policy was to reduce voluntary organizations' funds (through increases in VAT and reductions in the standard rate of taxation and therefore in the value of tax relief on charitable giving). Subsequently, these unintended consequences have been partially remedied: more generous provisions on tax relief were introduced in 1980. Similarly, the minimum period of covenanted giving has been reduced to four years. The estimated value of these concessions in the first full year was £30m, but the distribution of the sum is impossible to predict because of the uneven pattern of charitable giving. The longer-term effects of fiscal policies may be beneficial to the PSS field; the short-term effects were immediate and deleterious.

Direct support from the public purse — on which the Government is less keen — seems, at first glance, to have been more unequivocally helpful to the voluntary sector. Central government support has been maintained in real terms. However, under present protocols, central departments are confined to supporting national voluntary organizations and developments of national significance (the VSU-funded local initiatives experiment is seen as legitimately of national import). The role of local authority funding is therefore of great moment to the vitality of local voluntary services. This funding takes two main forms: grants-in-aid (and help in kind, e.g., with office space etc.); and the 'purchase' of service through agency agreements.

Central departments have not placed local authorities under great pressure to increase, or even maintain, grants-in-aid. The governance philosophy of minimal central intervention does seem to be taken seriously; reliance has been placed on the ministerial speech and exhortation. The Secretary of State has been sanguine about the success of this approach; voluntary organizations are seen to have received a measure of protection.[122] The problem of interpretation, however, is greatly complicated by the fluidity of boundary between much local statutory and voluntary activity. Faced, for example, by constraints on manpower, some local authorities have funded posts in voluntary organizations which might otherwise, or previously, have been located within the statutory sector.

Grants-in-aid, however, are not the whole story at local level, and voluntary organizations which 'sell' services — especially residential care — to local authorities face a more covert set of risks and pressures. While they have suffered loss of income from fiscal charges, their unit costs have been increasing. They have been under pressure from local authorities to absorb some element of these rising costs. This makes them extremely vulnerable to vacancy rates; they cannot afford to lose income on empty places. The pressure on local authorities, however, is to pursue a policy of 'internalization': to use their own facilities to the full and to limit their use of voluntary provision. There is localized evidence of rising vacancy rates in some voluntary organizations and of severe financial pressure.

The quality of government intelligence on these developments in the voluntary sector is unclear, though the House of Commons Social Services Committee was generally critical of the lack of monitoring of policy consequences.[123] There is certainly no reliable body of national data on how seriously voluntary organizations have been affected. The implementation of policy has been uneven and unsystematic to date and the outcome is unpredictable.

The formal voluntary organizations are not the heart of the matter, however. What influence has government on the *real* object of current thinking — the extension and strengthening of informal care? The most characteristic feature of informal care is that it is little understood; it has been long neglected by governments and academics alike. Without an established body of theory about the motivations of informal carers, how can governments devise policies to stimulate this form of care? Competing yet underdeveloped theories do exist; their implications for policy vary considerably.

Let us consider three by way of illustration. The first can be labelled 'state-induced altrusim'. The argument is that a sound infra-structure of free state services — state altruism — induces individuals to behave altrustically.[124] The message is obvious: protect state services. It is a thesis of limited appeal in present circumstances.

A second thesis is that patterns of social obligation and notions of 'group self-reliance' underpin informal care. Prevailing norms and values are therefore important, and the significance of state welfare is diminished or rendered ambiguous. The 'disengagement of the state' has been partly defended on the assumption that state services undermine social obligation: public expenditure cuts may themselves, in the extreme case, be seen as a means of promoting informal care. On this assumption, the Government could be seen as guilty of inadequate implementation: expenditure cuts have been insufficient. A potentially more direct approach to fostering a new ethic of social obligation has emerged briefly in heated exchanges on whether or not unemployed people should be pressured to engage in 'voluntary' community service. While a controversial and potentially embarrassing topic, it does indicate the range of direct measures which the Government could, but is not yet, deploying. It also highlights the fact that a 'language of social obligations' can imperceptibly replace the 'language of social rights' which dominated social policy until recently.

A third thesis raises even greater problems of policy implementation because it suggests a more sophisticated view of the interaction between statutory and non-statutory, formal and informal, social welfare. This may be characterized by Seebohm's term 'interweaving'.[125] Bayley provided evidence of the extent to which formal social services could be irrelevant to, or even weaken, informal patterns of coping.[126] But he also emphasised that the problem of implementation is to ensure that formal services do in fact reinforce informal caring. The need is for knowledge founded in systematic research, and for appropriate organizational structures and professional practices.

That the Government was content to exhort local authorities and voluntary organizations to support informal caring did seem to arise from a philosophical unwillingness to intervene more directly. But it also reflected a lack of detail; precisely *how* the role of formal services should change was far from clear. For example, Patrick Jenkin urged local authority social services departments to realise the 'enabling' role identified in the Seebohm Report:

SSDs should ensure that the full range of services are available locally by encouraging the use of all resources in all forms and by providing a basis of financial, administrative and professional support. This is quite different from actually providing all the services yourselves. In the simplest terms it consists of making sure that things happen and helping other people to make them happen.[127]

He supported this argument with a plea that social services committees should review their policies to examine whether 'the harnessing of voluntary and community resources' was central to their concerns and whether their policies were 'assisting a comprehensive, community-based approach to social care'. Directors of social services were asked to ascertain whether their staffs were 'ensuring that their clients [were] making the fullest possible use of caring resources available in their local communities'.[128] The social work profession was also urged to review its methods of work by considering whether the harnessing of community resources was fully reflected in the concept of casework and whether professional training adequately developed appropriate skills and perspectives. It was, no doubt, anticipated that the (Barclay) enquiry into social work would place such questions at the centre of much of its deliberations and may have been considered an opportunity for changes in professional training consonant with present Government policies.

However, that the existing body of ministerial exhortation lacked the cutting edge of a new and concrete model of service provision was candidly acknowledged by the Secretary of State in September 1980. While warmly commending the 'patch' system of organizing the deploying social services staff, he noted:

My colleagues and I have been seeking to argue that care in the community must mean care *by* the community. We have sought, sometimes not very successfully, to express this in a variety of ways . . . [Patch systems] seem to me to clothe with reality the concepts for which we have been groping.[129]

The new philosophy was most vividly brought to life — at least for the Secretary of State — in the guise of a particular means of implementing it.

Policy interaction and policy implementation. Any attempt to stimulate non-statutory social services poses problems of implementation, but they should not be exaggerated. The traditional panoply of discussion documents, white papers, circulars, planning guidelines and professional advice from the 'inspectorate' (the Social Work Service) could be used to promote an increase in local authority financial and professional support for non-statutory agencies and informal carers. Central government financial support and incentives to voluntary organizations could also be increased, while fiscal policy could be consistently used to swell funds. Finally, changes in professional training could be encouraged so as to promote new skills and values. That kind of integrated programmatic response had yet to emerge by December 1980 — or had been permanently eschewed. The picture of policy implementation which had emerged in practice up to that point was characterized by only limited activity and a real degree of inconsistency. The inconsistency, as we have seen, arose primarily from the impact of fiscal and public expenditure policies on social policies, but that did not make it unavoidable. A 'joint approach' to government social policy is as necessary when pursuing a minimalist strategy which emphasises the role of the non-statutory sector as it is when state services are to the fore.

The limited amount of implementation activity arose from the ambiguity of service policies, as well as from the constraints imposed by resource and governance policies. The DHSS was temporarily marooned on a foreign shore: old certainties were challenged and traditional mechanisms of influence and control at least partially immobilized. The ministerial speech filled the gap and perhaps became more influential for that very reason. But we have also noted the first signs of what may become a more active pursuit of specific developments. The Home Office moved onto the initiative in an experimental, if limited, way and Patrick Jenkin identified a congenial model of social service organization in the patch system. Despite the massive inertial force of 'disengagement' and expenditure restraint, some small wheels were turning in new directions by late 1980. Whether they were turning in compatible directions had, however, yet to become clear.

VI Conclusion

In reviewing the Government's expenditure plans in 1980, the Social Services Select Committee was greatly concerned about the apparent lack of coherent processes for strategic policy-making within the DHSS. In particular, it was critical of the Department's 'failure to examine the overall impact of changes in expenditure levels and changes in the social environment across the various services and programmes for which the department is responsible'.[130] Our discussion has also noted a number of apparent inconsistencies, contradictions and conflicts in Government policy towards the PSS. Examples include protecting the NHS from expenditure 'cuts' while selecting the closely interdependent PSS for the largest proportional 'cuts' of all LA services; increasing joint financing monies while reducing the ability of SSDs to commit themselves to such expenditure; encouraging a greater use of volunteers while calling for reductions in the number of public sector employees; seeking to attain a major shift in the balance between statutory and non-statutory forms of welfare while being committed to a reduction of central government intervention in local affairs.

We have identified such apparent inconsistencies not as evidence of the need to improve intra- and inter-departmental strategic policy co-ordination, though this is of undoubted importance to any government which wishes to enhance the impact of its policies. Rather, we have attempted to identify the existence of and inter-relationships between various streams of policy. Our argument is that it would be naive to search for a coherent body of service policy and to ask: how are these policies being implemented? The reality consists of divergence and conflict within the three policy streams which we have identified, as well as between them. Moreover, this very lack of congruence between policies also complicates and impedes their implementation. Tensions and contradictions between governance, resource and service policy streams, and between those and similar streams in related policy fields, arise in the lifetime of all governments. However, two features of this Government are perhaps unique in recent history. Firstly, it came to office determined to hold and then progressively reduce public expenditure. Secondly, it was committed to carrying through a minimalist philosophy of governance in the personal social services. This demanded both a more limited role for statutory provision and a disavowal of an interventionist stance in pursuit of that or any other end.

One area of uncertainty and confusion, that of policy towards non-statutory care, can reasonably be explained by the novelty of the problem it poses. Clear objectives take time to develop in any new field of thought and action. However, we have highlighted the importance attached to resource and governance objectives because it has had a more general effect. It has largely precluded the development of service policy initiatives and has also called into question the viability and meaning of inherited service policies. Our argument is that an absence of clarity about policy intent in one policy stream is a direct consequence of the pre-eminence given to the other two. However, we have also emphasised that this phenomenon is not new. Expenditure constraint during the lifetime of previous administrations had already seriously undermined the integrity of 'community care' as a policy. We have also suggested that the form of implementation adopted in the past — detailed, centralized planning of resource inputs — may have deflected attention from service objectives.[131]

Viewed from the present Government's own perspective, however, the internal inconsistencies of resource policies may be more worrying than the relative obscurity of service objectives. We are thinking particularly of resource restraint decisions which threaten to reduce cost-effectiveness by transferring demand to more expensive modes of care, by inhibiting the development of low-cost alternatives, and by inflating unmet need in the future.

The resource policy stream has also exposed interesting issues of implementation. Discussion of expenditure policy implementation has largely been based upon a presumption that 'cuts' were being 'imposed' on local authorities. It has also been based upon a quite indiscriminate use of the term 'cuts'. The evidence of real growth taking place could, therefore, appear to justify the Secretary of State's reference to 'hysterical' reactions. Yet it would be as over-simplistic to assert that no cuts were occurring as it would be to state the contrary. Our 'typology of cuts' is an attempt to introduce a measure of conceptual clarity into the debate and to demonstrate that certain kinds of cuts may take place even given expenditure growth. The PSS lobbies, if they are to retain credibility in government, must make clear what kind of cuts they are talking about. The consequences of crying wolf too often — or too soon — should not be underestimated. If resource pressures on the PSS do increase in the future, it may prove difficult to recreate even that degree of interest in and sympathy for the PSS which the lobbies were able to orchestrate during 1979 and 1980.

In the meantime, it appears that, generally speaking, local authorites have given some measure of protection to the PSS. Whether this represents the successful implementation of Government policy is a debatable point given the emphasis on the indicative nature of the figures for the distri-bution of expenditure between services — though expenditure White Papers do state that these represent the Government's view of national priorities. Patrick Jenkin, having endured the opprobrium which he incurred for agreeing to the White Paper figures, was subsequently moved to claim some share in the credit for the failure of local authorities to implement them:

> What has happened, *as I always suspected it would,* and I have welcomed this, is that local authorities have spent rather more on personal social services than the indicative figures in the White Paper had suggested. They are perfectly entitled to do that provided overall each local authority keeps within the government's target.[132]

If we accept this statement as anything more than a piece of post hoc justification, we must also note that contradictions within and between policy streams may not necessarily be unintended. Whether the PSS community would accept this explanation for the apparent contradictions and confusion in the Government's actions is, of course, an altogether different matter.

Nonetheless, it is the governance stream of policy, rather than the service and resource streams, which raises the most intriguing questions for students both of the personal social services and of public administration. For the former group such questions include the following. Can SSDs be encouraged to give greater emphasis to their role as 'enablers' and less to that of service providers? If so, what will be the strengths and limitations of the resulting service patterns? To what extent can informal care systems provide standards and levels of care acceptable to their recipients, their carers, and the electorate at large? Precisely how can such systems be stimulated, strengthened and supported by the organized statutory and voluntary sectors? What is to be the role of organized voluntarism in the new order? Is it capable of a vigorous response to the new opportunities apparently offered to it? Finally, what part will the private sector be encouraged to play; how, if at all, are its standards to be monitored and controlled?

It is perhaps the other strand of governance policy — that of disengagement and the reaction against dirigism — which is of more interest to the student of public administration and which raises the most intriguing problems of policy implementation. We noted earlier that at least two broad approaches to policy implementation can be identified: direct and indirect strategies. We have also questioned elsewhere the appropriateness of a direct — especially a dirigiste — approach to implementation in the PSS.[133] The absence of a hierarchical relationship between locally governed services on the one hand and the centre on the other, together with the latter's relative ignorance of local supply and demand conditions, suggested to us the appropriateness of an indirect strategy of implementation. Our suggestion was that compliance at the periphery might more readily be secured by attempting to influence decisional premises of actors located there, rather than by prescribing unrealistically precise service inputs in circumstances of imperfect knowledge and control.

The inclinations of this Government appear to be consistent with the notion of an indirect approach to policy implementation. However, the approach adopted so far has primarily revolved around the use of the ministerial speech — especially in the field of non-statutory care. It is unclear whether this represents a short term hiatus while a knowledge base is developed, instruments devised and programmes constructed which are consistent with governance policy. Alternatively, it may be that the philosophy of governance will be interpreted in terms so minimalist as to preclude DHSS from taking any initiatives beyond general exhortations to promote non-statutory welfare. If so, the role of the centre in policy development terms would be confined to the creation of 'a policy climate' within which each locality would be encouraged to develop its own strategy. But it would be surprising if central government took no other action to promote non-statutory welfare. The 1980 Finance Act, the modification of the urban aid programme[134] and the experimental development initiatives sponsored by the VSU were indications of moves towards a more active and programmatic approach. It is true that those initiatives were not sponsored by the DHSS, and it will be interesting to observe whether the philosophy of governance is interpreted differently in different departments or whether the relative inactivity of the DHSS merely represented a 'breathing space' while the Department geared itself up to adopt a more positive role.

It would certainly not be impossible to develop a more active strategy of implementation without doing violence to the present philosophy of governance by working through and in conjunction with, for example, the media, local authority associations, chairmen and directors of social services, the organized voluntary sector, the CBI, the TUC and the churches. Such activity could well have the limited objective of engaging such groups in discussion, developing ideas about ways in which the Government's broad principles might be translated into action and carrying such ideas through on an experimental basis. This would all be a long way from dirigism, but it would offer opportunities for shaping the assumptive worlds of individuals at the centre and the periphery and for developing a variety of approaches to the promotion of non-statutory welfare.

Finally, in view of all the rhetoric about rolling back the boundaries of the public sector, it is worth noting that the immediate reality has been very much more modest in the PSS. No fundamental surgery has been proposed for the PSS — no major functions have been taken away from them. Nonetheless, it is not inconceivable that the lifetime of this Government will see a significant change in the role of SSDs. The combination of demand pressures, resource shortages and central government encouragement for alternatives to statutory service provision may force SSDs increasingly to view their role in 'enabling' terms. The forthcoming report of the Barclay Committee may have an important influence, leading the social work profession in the same direction. Conflicting and apparently inconsistent policies may affect change as readily as coherent and systematically implemented plans.

References

Preface

1 P.M. Jackson (ed.), *Government Policy Initiatives 1979-80: Some Case Studies in Public Administration* (London: Royal Institute of Public Administration, 1981).

I

2 Royal Commission on the National Health Service, *Report,* Cmnd 7615 (London: HMSO, 1979), p. 435. For an analysis of expenditure trends in the PSS during the 1970s, see A.L. Webb and G. Wistow, 'The Personal Social Services: Incrementalism, Expediency or Systematic Social Planning?', in A. Walker (ed.), *Public Expenditure and Social Priorities* (London: Heinemann, 1981).

3 A. Webb, L. Day, and D. Weller, *Voluntary Social Service Manpower Resources* (London: Personal Social Services Council, 1976), p. 5.

4 Wolfenden Committee: *The Future of Voluntary Organisations* (London: Croom Helm, 1977), p. 36.

5 R.A. Pinker, *Research Priorities in the Personal Social Services* (London: Social Science Research Council, 1978), p. 47.

II

6 See, for example, leading articles in *Community Care,* 6 March 1980 and 7 August 1980. See also E. Cassam, 'Yours Very Confused', *Community Care,* 31 July 1980, p. 29.

7 Social Services Committee Third Report, Session 1979-80, *The Government's White Papers on Public Expenditure: The Social Services* (London: HMSO, 1980), H.C. 702-I.

8 P. Self, *Administrative Theories and Politics* (London: Allen & Unwin, 1972).

III

9 Social Services Committee 1979-80, para. 29.

10 A. Etzioni, *A Comparative Analysis of Complex Organizations* (New York: Free Press, 1961).

11 K. Judge, *Rationing Social Services* (London: Heinemann, 1978).

12 The interaction of the values of individuals, government, commercial and non-commercial institutions in housing policy provides useful examples of differential salience accorded to objectives and lack of congruence between the assumptive worlds of participants in a policy system. See G. Wistow, 'Managing Housing Policy — The Implementation of Policy in the Owner Occupied Sector', *Local Government Studies,* October 1978, pp. 53-66.

13 A.L. Webb and G. Wistow, 'Implementation, Central-Local Relations and the Personal Social Services', in George Jones (ed.) *New Approaches to the Study of*

Central-Local Government Relationships (Farnborough: Gower, 1980). The term 'banner goals' is used by Algie to describe 'grand abstractions which satisfy the condition of being what everyone would want for everyone . . . summing up concepts embodied in the grand design which represents the agency's philosophy.' J. Algie, *Social Values, Objectives and Action* (London: Kogan Page, 1975), p. 23.

14 P. Townsend; *The Last Refuge* (London: Routledge and Kegan Paul, 1962).

15 National Development Group for the Mentally Handicapped, *Pamphlets 1-5* (DHSS, 1977) and *Helping Mentally Handicapped People in Hospitals* (DHSS, 1978).

16 DHSS, *Priorities in the Health and Personal Social Services* (London: HMSO, 1976) and DHSS: *The Way Forward* (London: HMSO, 1977).

17 A. Wildavsky, 'Rescuing Policy Analysis from PPBS', *Public Administration Review,* vol. XXIX, March/April 1969, pp. 189-202.

IV

18 *The Conservative Manifesto* (London: Conservative Central Office, 1979), p. 6.

19 *Conservative Manifesto,* p. 7 (original emphasis).

20 A term initially used in a speech by Sir George Young, Parliamentary Under-Secretary for Health, to describe the desired relationship between central government and the NHS in the 1980s. (See report in *Health and Social Services Journal,* 2 May 1980, p. 568.) It appears to be equally applicable to central-local relations in the PSS.

21 'Statement by Mr. Patrick Jenkin', DHSS Press Notice 80/201, 5 August 1980.

22 Patrick Jenkin, speech to Personal Social Services conference, 21 November 1979.

23 *Controls in Local Government,* Cmnd 7634 (London: HMSO, 1979).

24 The number of circulars sent by DHSS to the NHS and to local authorities was reduced from 247 in 1978/79 to 69 in 1980/81. Social Services Committee Third Report, Session 1980/81: *Public Expenditure on the Social Services,* HC 324, volume II (London: HMSO, 1981), p. 124.

25 DHSS, *DHSS Planning Guidelines for 1980/81,* HC(80)9 (DHSS, July 1980), p. 1.

26 Social Services Committee 1980-81, vol. I. para. 51.

27 William Whitelaw, speech to the Liverpool Council of Social Service, 9 May 1980.

28 Whitelaw, speech to Liverpool Council of Social Service.

29 Patrick Jenkin, speech to an Age Concern conference, 7 February 1980.

30 Jenkin, speech to Age Concern.

31 Jenkin, speech to Personal Social Services conference.

32 'Jenkin On Cuts', *Social Work Today,* vol. 11, no. 9, 30 October 1979, p. 10.

33 The relationship between the experience (or threat) of unemployment and the incidence of physical and mental illness has become an issue of growing concern and controversy. See, for example, L. Fagin, *Unemployment and Health in Families* (London: HMSO, 1981); M. Colledge, *Unemployment and Health* (North Tyneside Community Health Council, 1981); Office of Health Economics (OHE), *Sickness Absence: A Review* (London: OHE, 1981). See also the *British Medical Journal,* May 1981 onwards, for a continuing series of articles by General Practitioners under the general title, 'Unemployment In My Practice'.

34 'Jenkin on Cuts', pp. 10-11.

35 Department of the Environment, *Local Authority Expenditure in 1979-80,* Circular 21/79 (DOE, July 1979), para. 3.

36 *The Government's Expenditure Plans 1980-81,* Cmnd 7746 (London: HMSO, 1979).

37 *Government's Expenditure Plans 1980-81,* para. 12.

38 *Government's Expenditure Plans 1980-81,* para. 12.

39 Personal Social Services Council, *The Way Forward: Comments by the Officers of the Personal Social Services Council* (PSSC, 1977).

40 *Government's Expenditure Plans 1980-81,* para. 38.

41 *The Government's Expenditure Plans 1980-81 to 1983-84,* Cmnd 7841 (London: HMSO, 1980).

42 *Parliamentary Debates,* 31 March 1980, col. 48.

43 Social Services Committee Third Report, Session 1979-80, *The Government's White Papers on Public Expenditure: The Social Services,* vol. II, Minutes of Evidence and Appendix (London: HMSO 1980), HC 702-II, pp. 36-37.

44 Patrick Jenkin, *Speech to the Residential Care Association (RCA),* 31 October 1979.

45 Jenkin, speech to Personal Social Services conference.

46 Social Services Committee 1979-80, p. 66.

47 Letter from Patrick Jenkin to MIND reported in *Community Care,* 22 November 1979, p. 5.

48 Social Services Committee 1979-80, para. 29.

49 For example, Association of Directors of Social Services, *Survey on Cuts/Savings in Social Services Expenditure: Interim Report,* October 1972; *Cuts in Public Expenditure: The Effects on the Personal Social Services,* February 1980; *Report of the Second Survey of the Extent and Effects of Cuts/Savings in Expenditure on the Personal Social Services,* September 1980; Personal Social Services Council, *Reductions in Local Authority Expenditure on the Personal Social Services: Paper Two: Further Developments 1979-80,* October 1979 and Paper Three: *Confirmation of Trends 1979-80 and 1980-81,* February 1980; Social Priorities Alliance, *Cuts in Local Authority Spending on Personal Social Services,* July 1980; *New Society,* 'Are the Local Authority Social Services Being Bled Dry?', 10 July 1980, pp. 59-62.

50 Association of Directors of Social Services, *Report of the Second Survey of the Extent and Effects of Cuts/Savings in Expenditure on the Personal Social Services* Newcastle upon Tyne, ADSS, 1980), pp. 1 and 11.

51 Personal Social Services Council (PSSC), *Reductions in Local Authority Expenditure on the Personal Social Services. Interim Paper 3: Confirmation of Trends* (PSSC, 1980), p. 3.

52 Jenkin, speech to Personal Social Services conference.

53 Jenkin, speech to RCA.

54 ADSS, *Report of the Second Survey,* pp. 1-2.

55 Social Priorities Alliance, *Cuts in Local Authority Spending on Personal Social Services,* July 1980, p. 25.

56 M. Cowan, 'Cuts Targets', *Municipal Journal,* 1 August 1980, p. 963

57 Figures given by Patrick Jenkin in speech to the ADSS conference, 19 September 1980.

58 ADSS, *Report of the Second Survey*, p. 82.

59 ADSS, *Report of the Second Survey*, p. 10.

60 Social Services Committee 1979-80, p. 144.

61 ADSS, *Report of the Second Survey*, p. 86.

62 Social Services Committee 1980-81, vol. II, pp. 6-9.

63 Calculated from Table 2.11, *The Government's Expenditure Plans 1981/82 to 1983/84*, Cmnd 8175 (London: HMSO, 1981), pp. 110-111.

64 Social Services Committee 1980-81, vol. II, pp. 6-9.

65 Chartered Institute of Public Finance and Accounting (CIPFA), *Personal Social Services Statistics: Actuals 1979/80* (CIPFA, 1981).

66 See ADSS, *Report of the Second Survey*, p. 6 and PSSC, *Reductions in Local Authority Expenditure*, p. 6. Other authorities were reported to be reducing simultaneously residential and community care service, however.

67 ADSS, *Report of the Second Survey*, p. 6; PSSC *Reductions in Local Authority Expenditure*, pp. 5-6. Unlike the case of children, there was no evidence of authorities explicitly closing residential facilities for the elderly in order to provide additional resources to develop community services.

68 Provisional figures presented to the Select Committee on Social Services by the DHSS for all English authorities show an increase in 1979/80 of 1.4% in the number of occupied places in residential homes for the elderly compared with the reduction of 0.7% in the number of elderly persons 'in care' in the CIPFA statistics. The same source shows the number of day care places for the elderly (about which CIPFA gives no information) to have increased by 6.4%. See Social Services Committee 1980-81 vol. II, p. 106.

69 Social Services Committee 1980-81, vol. II, p. 139.

70 Webb and Wistow, 'The Personal Social Services'.

71 Jenkin, speech to Personal Social Services conference.

72 Cassam, 'Yours Very Confused'.

73 Jenkin, speech to ADSS conference.

74 Judge, for example, concluded on the basis of what was acknowledged to be imperfect evidence that 'a substantial proportion of authorities do pay close heed to central government financial guidance'. K. Judge, 'The Financial Relationship Between Central and Local Government in the Personal Social Service', in T.A. Booth (ed.), *Planning for Welfare* (Oxford: Basil Blackwell and Martin Robertson, 1979).

75 *Young Offenders*, Cmnd 8045 (London: HMSO, 1980).

76 Letter from Patrick Jenkin to Professor Peter Mittler (Chairman of National Development Group), 10 June 1980, attached to National Development Group, *Unfinished Business*, mimeo, May 1980.

77 The review was eventually published in December 1980 under the title *Mental Handicap: Progress, Problems and Priorities* (London: DHSS, 1980).

78 DHSS, *A Happier Old Age* (London: HMSO, 1978). The commitment to publish a White Paper in 1980 was given by Patrick Jenkin in his speech to Age Concern in

February 1980. The White Paper first appeared in March 1981 in *Growing Older,* Cmnd 8173 (London: HMSO, 1981).

79 National Development Group, *Unfinished Business,* para. 18.

80 The limitations of joint finance in a climate of general resource constraint were underlined by the findings of a survey conducted by the National Association of Health Authorities in the Spring of 1981. Sixty percent of AHAs reported that their associated local authorities were placing restrictions on the use of joint finance because of financial constraints. See G. Wistow and S. Head, 'Pump Priming Programme', *Health and Social Services Journal,* 3 July 1981, pp. 806-807; and G. Wistow and S. Head, *Financing Community Care: Views From The Grassroots* (Department of Social Sciences, University of Loughborough, 1981).

81 A consultative document on possible ways of transferring patients and resources from the NHS to the PSS was published in July 1981. DHSS, *Care in the Community* (London: DHSS, 1981).

82 Personal Social Services Council, *The Future of the Personal Social Services* (London: PSSC, 1979), para. 25-26.

83 National Health Service Act 1980, Social Security Act (No. 1) 1979, Social Security Act (No. 2) 1980. For a fuller discussion of the implications of NHS restructuring for collaboration with local government, see G. Wistow and A. Webb: *Patients First: One Step Backwards for Collaboration?* (Department of Social Sciences, University of Loughborough, 1980).

84 Patrick Jenkin's letter of introduction to *Care In Action* (London: HMSO, 1981).

V

85 Jenkin, speech to Age Concern.

86 Social Services Committee 1979-80, p. 102.

87 The expression 'the pure doctrine of state welfare' is used to represent the widespread acceptance —across both the helping professions, and within the large sections of 'educated opinion' and the media — of state, publicly funded, professional social services as an appropriate and effective response to many social ills. Support for this doctrine varied greatly and was strongest in the Labour Party, among social welfare academics, and some caring professions. The 'collapse' in this doctrine represents a far more widespread questioning of this earlier faith and a much greater willingness to question the cost to public funds of upholding it. The collapse has proceeded least quickly in the original strongholds of the doctrine, but even large sections of the Labour Party are more cost-conscious than used to be the case and more positive about the merits of alternatives and supplements to state social provision. This section is drawn from A.L. Webb, 'Voluntary Social Action: In Search of a Policy?', *Journal of Voluntary Action Research,* vol. 8, 1979.

88 *Report of the Committee on Local Authority and Allied Personal Social Services* (Seebohm Report), Cmnd 3703 (London: HMSO, 1968), p. 153.

89 Seebohm Report, p. 14.

90 M. Roof, *A Hundred Years of Family Welfare* (London: Michael Joseph, 1972).

91 Seebohm Report, p. 153.

92 G.M. Aves, *The Volunteer Worker in the Social Services* (London: George Allen and Unwin, 1969), ch. 3.

93 Aves, *Volunteer Worker,* ch. 3.

94 Aves, *Volunteer Worker,* pp. 35-7.

95 Aves, *Volunteer Worker,* p. 87.

96 See R.A. Parker, unpublished Inaugural Lecture, University of Bristol, 1970; R.M. Titmuss, *The Gift Relationship* (London: Allen and Unwin, 1970); R. Hadley, A. Webb and C. Farrell, *Across the Generations* (London: George Allen and Unwin, 1975); P. Abrams, 'Community Care: Some Research Problems and Priorities', *Policy and Politics,* vol. 6, pp. 125-153, 1977; P. Abrams; *Neighbourhood Care and Social Policy: a research perspective* (Berkhamsted, Herts: The Volunteer Centre, 1978); D. Leat, *Why Volunteers?* (Berkhamsted, Herts: The Volunteer Centre, 1978).

97 A.A. Goodman, *Charity Law and Voluntary Organisations* (London: Bedford Square Press, 1976).

98 Wolfenden Committee, ch. 2.

99 Wolfenden Committee, p. 36.

100 Webb, et al., *Voluntary Social Service Manpower.*

101 Home Office, *The Government and the Voluntary Sector: A Consultative Document* (London: Home Office, 1978).

102 National Council of Voluntary Organisations (NCVO), *Beyond The Welfare State* (NCVO, 1980). The critique presented here of the NCVO's case is drawn from A. Webb, *Collective Action and Welfare Pluralism,* a paper given to the AGM of the Association of Researchers in Voluntary Action and Community Involvement (ARVAC), 12 December 1980. A revised version of that paper is available as ARVAC Occasional Paper No. 3 (Wivenhoe, Essex, 1981).

103 B. Davies, *The Cost-Effectiveness Imperative, The Social Services and Volunteers* (Berkhamsted, Herts.: The Volunteer Centre, 1980).

104 Roy Parker, 'Tending and Social Policy' in T. Goldberg and S. Hatch (eds.), *A New Look at the Personal Social Services* (London: Policy Studies Institute, 1981).

105 Philip Abrams, 'Community Care: Some Research Problems and Policies', *Policy and Politics* 6, 2, December 1977.

106 Wolfenden Committee and F. Gladstone, *Voluntary Action in a Changing World* (London: Bedford Square Press, 1980).

107 Wolfenden Committee.

108 Wolfenden Committee.

109 A recent study illustrated this point most effectively when it asked: 'Do we seriously want . . . to follow . . . decentralisation to its logical conclusion and decentralise to authorities where another in the depressing list of scandals in long-stay hospitals has recently erupted?' S. Haywood and A. Alaszewski, *Crisis in the Health Service* (London: Croom Helm, 1981).

110 For a more detailed discussion of these issues see Wistow and Webb, *Patients First.*

111 M. Brenton, 'Getting a Grip on the Dutch Voluntary Sector', *Voluntary Action,* Spring 1980.

112 Gladstone, *Voluntary Action.*

113 *Conservative Manifesto,* p. 27.

114 Merlyn Rees, Preface to *The Government and the Voluntary Sector: A Consultative Document* (London: HMSO 1976), p. ii (emphasis added).

115 Jenkin, speech to ADSS.

116 Jenkin, speech to ADSS (emphasis added).

117 Bill Utting, 'Changing Ways of Caring', *Health and Social Services Journal*, 4 July 1980, p. 882.

118 Jenkin, speech to Age Concern.

119 NCVO, *Beyond the Welfare State*.

120 Jenkin, speech to ADSS.

121 Jenkin, speech to ADSS.

122 Jenkin, speech to ADSS. Jenkin's comments were based upon the findings of the ADSS survey that only 14 of 78 authorities responding to the survey made 'cuts/savings' in grants to voluntary bodies. Thirty-five of the 78 authorities made no response to this question. ADSS, *Report of the Second Survey*.

123 Social Services Committee 1979-80.

124 See R.A. Pinker, *The Idea of Welfare* (London: Heinemann, 1979) and Titmuss, *The Gift Relationship*.

125 Seebohm Report, para. 483.

126 M. Bayley, *Mental Handicap and Community Care* (London: Routledge and Kegan Paul, 1973).

127 Jenkin, speech to ADSS.

128 Jenkin, speech to ADSS.

129 Patrick Jenkin's speech to the 'Patch Workshop' held at the National Institute of Social Work on 15 September 1980.

VI

130 Social Services Committee 1979-80, para. 15.

131 See Webb and Wistow, 'Implementation, Central-Local Relations, and the Personal Social Services'.

132 Social Services Committee 1980-81, vol. II, p. 138 (emphasis added).

133 Webb and Wistow, 'Implementation, Central-Local Relations, and the Personal Social Services'.

134 The 1980 Urban Aid Circular emphasised that high priority should be given to voluntary sector schemes. DOE Circular 15/80, Department of the Environment, September 1980.

About the Authors

Adrian Webb and Gerald Wistow are, respectively, Professor and Research Fellow in Social Administration at the University of Loughborough. They are members of the RIPA research group examining the implementation of policy initiatives undertaken by the Conservative Government elected in 1979 and contributed to the group's first interim report. They are currently working with the RIPA and the University of Bath on a major research project on the coordination of social policy at central and local levels of government.

The authors' previous joint publications have included papers on central-local relations in the personal social services, the potential consequences of NHS restructuring for collaboration between health and local authorities, and the impact of public expenditure trends in the personal social services on the development of community care. They are currently writing a book on joint planning and joint finance based on recently completed empirical work on health and local authorities.

Adrian Webb is the joint author of *Change, Choice and Conflict in Social Policy* (Heinemann, 1975), *Across the Generations: Old People and Young Volunteers* (Allen and Unwin, 1975) and joint editor of *Teamwork in the Personal Social Services and Health Care* (Croom Helm, 1980). He has written widely about management, research and policy in the personal social services in both the statutory and non-statutory sectors. He is the Chairman of the Volunteer Centre. Gerald Wistow has published papers on the implementation of housing policy, health and local authority collaboration, and the financing of community care.